Praise for
How to Become a Black Writer

"Marita Golden is a living and breathing gift to America, and to this world, through her writing, teaching, and helping of others. Marita Golden's journey has been one of communion and community, of literature and the search for freedom for herself, and for all people. With her new book *How to Become a Black Writer*, Marita Golden presents us with a text that is a virtual master class: it is part memoir, part history, and part meditation on race, gender, identity, and how we can be seen and heard and felt when there are those trying to erase our voices, our books, our history."

> —Kevin Powell, Grammy-nominated
>   poet and author of sixteen books

"Marita Golden is a giant of American literature. Also boasting a small stature, I've often wondered how all that creativity and fierceness is squeezed into only five feet of brilliant Black woman. Her exquisite fiction and nonfiction have loomed large in my mind."

> —Kwame Alexander, #1 *New York Times*
>   bestselling author of forty books and
>   Emmy Award-winning producer

"*How to Become a Black Writer* is the book I wish someone had handed me when I was starting out on the writer's journey. Part intimate memoir, part living history (Eldridge Cleaver! Toni Morrison! Audre Lorde!) and part love letter to the power of storytelling and the vital necessity of art for Black people, this book would have saved me valuable time and artistic loneliness. Through her storied career, her peerless teaching and her ceaseless activism and institution building, Marita Golden has already done more for Black literature and Black writers than anyone has the right to ask. With this wise and witty volume—this covering, this gift to us—she has somehow done even more."

—Kimberly McLarin, author of *Everyday Something Has Tried to Kill Me and Has Failed*

"In *How to Become a Black Writer*, award-winning author and institution builder Marita Golden takes us on an empowering and resourceful personal journey to discover the sorcery of words and the magic that attends her deep love of Black stories and Black lives."

—Joanne V. Gabbin, founder of the Furious Flower Poetry Center and founder and executive director of the Wintergreen Women Writers Collective

How to Become a
Black Writer

Other Books by Marita Golden

Migrations of the Heart

Long Distance Life

After

A Woman's Place

The Edge of Heaven

And Do Remember Me

*Wild Women Don't Wear No
Blues: Black Women Writers
on Love, Men and Sex*

*The Word: Black Writers Talk
About the Transformative
Power of Reading and Writing*

*Us Against Alzheimer's:
Stories of Family,
Love, and Faith*

The Wide Circumference of Love

*It's All Love: Black Writers on
Soul Mates, Family, and Friends*

*Don't Play in the Sun:
One Woman's Journey
Through the Color Complex*

*Skin: An Interactive Journal
for Women Who Want to
Heal the Color Complex*

*Skin Deep: Black Women
& White Women
Write About Race*

*Gumbo: An Anthology of
African American Writing*

*A Miracle Every Day:
Triumph and Transformation
in the Lives of Single Mothers*

*Saving Our Sons:
Raising Black Children
in a Turbulent World*

*First Page to Finished:
On Writing and Living
the Writer's Life*

*The Strong Black Woman:
How a Myth Endangers
the Physical and Mental
Health of Black Women*

*The New Black Woman:
Loves Herself, Has Boundaries,
and Heals Every Day*

How to Become a
Black Writer

*Creating and Honoring
Black Stories
That Matter*

MARITA GOLDEN

Miami

For permission requests, please contact the publisher at:

Mango Publishing Group

5966 South Dixie Highway, Suite 300

Miami, FL 33143

info@mango.bz

For special orders, quantity sales, course adoptions and corporate sales, please email the publisher at sales@mango.bz. For trade and wholesale sales, please contact Ingram Publisher Services at customer.service@ingramcontent.com or +1.800.509.4887.

How to Become a Black Writer: Creating and Honoring Black Stories That Matter

Library of Congress Cataloging-in-Publication Number: 2024947375

ISBN: (print) 978-1-68481-715-3, (ebook) 978-1-68481-716-0

BISAC: BIO022000, BIOGRAPHY & AUTOBIOGRAPHY / Women

Printed in the United States of America

Table of Contents

Foreword

I spent the first ten years of my writing life trying to be Langston Hughes because of one essay. It was classic Langston: bold and correct, harsh and funny. He called it *How to Be a Bad Writer*. Published over a half century ago, it is a wonder (and a sorrow) that its literary lessons still ring true. This, of course, is the phenomenon that defines Langston Hughes: the ability to speak truth that lasts, an inherent remembering of one man's words that moves beyond all circumstance, a small Black man with a timeless knack for making folks the world over laugh to keep from crying.

Marita Golden is a giant of American literature. Also boasting a small stature, I've often wondered how all that creativity and fierceness is squeezed into only five feet of brilliant Black woman. Her exquisite fiction and nonfiction have loomed large in my mind since I fell in love with her autobiography, *Migrations of the Heart*, a year out of college, and wished that one day I might write something so authentic, so activist, so interesting.

A day before I won the Newbery Medal for the most distinguished contribution to American literature for children, an award that would change my life, I sat in her basement with three other ambitious writers, all of us drafting poems and prose in the moments between asking her questions, listening to her stories, and being fed her chicken salad sandwiches and encouragement. We were hungry for Marita's advice and inspiration, her respect and mentorship, and she gave it to us, in doses we could handle. Then she'd collect our plates and go back upstairs to her study to write. We prayed we would one day ascend to those heights, but we were just happy to know that the mere fact that we were in her home meant that some of her excellence just might rub off on us.

As I've matured in my writing, two things have become clear to me. First, a good writer must be courageous enough to share the soul eternal, to speak truth to the people. Secondly, a great writer must write all the time, until the last bit of juice is squeezed from the lemon, and even then, she must find another lemon. This is the sweetness of life that Marita Golden continues to show us.

She says this book is a how-to. It is, but it's also more. It's memoir and craft lesson. It's autobiography and cultural manifesto. This book you're holding in your hand is a companion, maybe even a sequel, to Langston's seminal essay. *How to Become a Black Writer* is a vivid and vibrant snapshot of a thirty-plus-year writerly life filled with all the things you need to write a successful narrative, tell your story true, and be excellent all at the same time. It doesn't get more interesting than that.

—Kwame Alexander

Introduction

The seeds of this book were planted on Thursday, December 7, 2023, which was officially declared Marita Golden Day in my hometown of Washington, DC, and in Prince George's County, Maryland, a DC suburb where I live. On that day I was honored for my writing and literary activism in an intimate, deeply moving ceremony at the Martin Luther King Jr. Memorial Library, the central library in DC's city-wide twenty-six location system. The celebration and all its large and small components were organized by several members of my writing "sister circle," women writers whose friendship I cherish and whose talent I applaud—women whom I have mentored and whom I am continually learning from. Creating and sustaining networks of support for writers has been an enduring endeavor for me, one that is in many ways foundational to my sense of self.

That December day was nearing the close of a year that had held considerable importance for me, as it marked the fortieth anniversary of the 1983 publication of my first book, my memoir, *Migrations of the Heart*. I had been in a celebratory mood since the beginning of the year, quietly and without much fanfare nurturing a deep satisfaction, because I knew the significance of the fact that forty years after my first book, I was still writing and publishing, still teaching and mentoring writers, still encouraging literary activism.

Writers Abdul Ali and Tracy Chiles McGhee interviewed me on Zoom as part of the online program "I Dreamed A World" to note this fortieth-anniversary publishing milestone, and I hosted a party with two dozen members of the writer's "sister circle" to honor all of us. These were events that I organized—in the words of Walt Whitman—to "celebrate myself."

So, I was surprised and enormously gratified when Tracy informed me that she and several other writers were planning an event to honor me. On that day, writers and others came together, including many I had taught or mentored, people with whom I had worked on literary projects, and honorees of the Hurston/Wright Foundation, which I cofounded, to offer testimonies to the impact of my writing, teaching, and activism. This was the kind of day writers often fear they will not live long enough to witness—the kind of day that feels both triumphant and humbling. Several times, as I watched friends offer accounts attesting to the fact that I had lived both an examined and vibrantly created life, I nearly wept. I did weep after a breathtaking dramatization of a monologue I had written to capture the voice of Harriet Tubman in my book *The Strong Black Woman*, a performance passionately rendered by multi-genre artist and actor Pamela Woolford. That day was forty years in the making. The search for communion and community has long activated my writing. That day confirmed that I had both designed and found the community I had yearned for.

In the days and weeks following that afternoon of fellowship, I felt a slowly evolving but insistent desire to write about my writing life and career. In day and night dreams,

I appraised the past forty years as though they belonged to and had been lived by someone else. That objectivity convinced me to write this meditation, this narrative, this history in the making. I found and harnessed my writer's voice and consciousness during one of the most significant eras in American literary culture, the 1970s, '80s, and '90s, three decades in which Black women writers expanded the American literary canon and worked to lay to rest some of the most damaging and enduring stereotypes about Black life in America. That work continues today, but those decades shaped me and continue to influence the Black excellence in writing unfolding today. This is an important story about political and social change, the impact of literature, and evidence of how African Americans revolutionize and often humanize everything we touch. I wrote my first poetry as a Negro girl and my memoir as a Black woman.

I've written this ode to the act of writing for readers, writers, writers yet to realize that's who they are, writers unborn, and everyone who has learned how to breathe and to be as a result of the art of the story. That's all of us. How to write a successful narrative, one that engages the reader, provokes emotions, and enlarges the reader's world, is a sublime mystery: a mystery that writers seek to solve again and again. Every book I've written was an assignment from God, a spark from the Big Bang, fingerprinted by quantum physics. Writing begins as a Rubik's cube of possibilities, questions, and puzzles. One of my greatest joys in life is to work with the clay of all of that. In this book I am honoring people, but I am also honoring process, persistence, dedication, and hard work.

Leo Tolstoy, Zora Neale Hurston, Mary Oliver, Richard Wright, Frederick Douglass and a global constellation of past and present writers have inspired and continue to inspire me. A story well-told is a bridge into the heart of the writer and their world: a bridge that eradicates barriers to empathy and connection. A Black story is a life story as universal as Faulkner's *As I Lay Dying* is assumed by all to be. We are all the default setting for humanity. By the end of this narrative, I hope you realize, as have I, that telling a Black life story, imagining a Black life story, and telling that story true is an act of heroism. Just think about the wondrous depth of the literary genetic code connecting W.E.B. DuBois and Octavia Butler, William Wells Brown, and Toni Morrison to the rivers Langston Hughes knew. Each book I have written taught me how to write it. I have been a student and a master of the text. I've always written to be read. This time I'm writing to inspire. Come, take my hand...

> *"But my interest is in how these marks that I am scratching on this page can mean anything at all. If they can have meaning, then life can have meaning, then I can have meaning."*
>
> —Percival Everett, *James*

> *"Art is somewhat of a prayer, isn't it?"*
> —Actor Bill Cobb

CHAPTER ONE

The Girl Who Flew on the Wings of Words

I am nine years old, lying beneath the blanket in my twin-sized bed. A dull prick of light shimmers in the room's darkness as I eagerly resist sleep, waiting to be transported. Soon my bedroom will become a stage. My father sits beside me in a straight-back chair. The scent of his cigar-scented skin pulls me close. My father's skin is dark. Dark like night. Yet I see him inside the shadows that fill the room as he clears his throat, the signal that a story is about to begin.

Tonight, the story is about a woman named Harriet Tubman—a woman who was enslaved. My father often takes me on nocturnal expeditions to meet Black people who made and changed history. These are people I often have not learned about in school. They are men and women who under the spell of my father's voice and words I imagine and see on the walls and the ceiling of my room, loving their families, running to freedom, standing tall and brave in the soil of this place called *history* that my father makes real for me on nights like this.

I have met Benjamin Banneker, a free man when most Black people were not, a mathematician and astronomer who helped design Washington, DC, where my family lives. I have met Phillis Wheatley who was kidnapped, enslaved, and brought from the Gambia in West Africa to America and wrote poems about the life she had been taken from and the life she had to make anew.

One night my father guided my fingers to touch the country of Egypt on a globe and showed me a photograph of the Sphinx, that country's and one of the world's most famous statues. My father tells me the Sphinx has my broad full nose. I catch my breath at the thought that people who look like me made such an enormous, grand thing.

But tonight, I meet Harriet Tubman, who escaped slavery and returned to the South many times to bring her family and others to freedom. My father is a wonderful storyteller, so I hear dogs barking furiously trying to pick up Tubman's scent as slave catchers search for her. Her fearful deep breaths pulse in the room as she hides in shallow creeks, traveling by night guided by the North Star. My stomach grumbles in hunger as she desperately searches for food in the marshes of the Eastern Shore of Maryland. Famished, afraid, determined, and faith-filled Harriet Tubman walks and runs almost one hundred miles to freedom. Intrepid and bold, she was a spy for the Union army during the Civil War and lead the Combahee River Raid that freed seven hundred enslaved people. A recognized hero in her own time, Tubman lived to be ninety-three years old. I fall asleep with Harriet Tubman and freedom on my mind.

These stories were my goodnight, my sleep tight. My father guided me along a historical underground railroad. Did my father know he was creating a writer? Did he know he was teaching me the elements of a good story? Of powerful storytelling and *writing*? A person is tested. An obstacle is overcome. Did he know he was teaching me how to be a sorcerer of language? On those storytelling nights, the people I met became my kin, the places he took me, my home.

Who was this man, my father, Francis Sherman Golden? He was black-black, and to my daughter's eyes, that Blackness was like his last name, like my last name: Golden. At a time when many hated to be Black or to be called Black, my father wore and lived his Blackness like an unfurled flag snapping in the wind. He was proud in a world that told him he had no reason to be.

I was born in 1950 into an America of visible and invisible lines of separation and segregation. In Washington, DC, there were Black schools, White schools, Black restaurants, White restaurants, Black movie theaters, and White movie theaters. The embrace of my family and community, however, meant that I did not grow up feeling there was anything I needed that I did not have.

We lived not far from U Street, the heartbeat of segregated Black DC, where we saw movies at theaters named for Paul Lawrence Dunbar, a Black writer who became famous for his poetry and stories, and Booker T. Washington, a formerly enslaved man who in post-Civil War Alabama founded Tuskegee Institute, a school that gave hope and training to many generations of Black people. Today, as Tuskegee University, that same school is now a prominent and thriving historically Black college.

On U Street, back then sometimes called "Black Broadway," Black people cut our hair, taught us business skills at Cortez Peters Business College, buried us at Lincoln Cemetery, loaned us money at Industrial Bank, performed at the Howard Theater, and saved our souls at one of the scores of Black churches ranging from Baptist to AME.

I was born into a world that was about to change because of real-life people who were very much like the ones my father told me about at bedtime: people loving their families, running for freedom, and standing tall and brave in the soil of this place called history, including Thurgood Marshall, Bayard Rustin, Coretta Scott King, Dr. Martin Luther King Jr., Pauli Murray, Angela Davis, Huey P. Newton, and Shirley Chisholm.

My father's accounts taught me that every day, somewhere in the world in the most unexpected of places, someone was born who was willing to fight for justice and challenge lies with truth. Those nightly narratives enabled me to fly into the world on the wings of words that could unlock secrets and rewrite and reclaim history.

The newspapers, *The Washington Post* and *The Evening Star*, were filled with words like integration, civil rights, and Freedom Riders. I asked my father what the words meant. He explained their meaning and that those words were spoken by people who wanted to make a new world. I would witness the once-thought-impossible changes that reshaped the world I was born into. I'd be shaped by political and social revolt, resistance, and reform and as a writer honor the legacies of the men and women whose blood, my father implied, ran through my veins.

* * *

My father made stories an important part of my life. I believed that imagination was good and necessary, and so I became a daydreaming girl, always writing a story or a poem or imagining a play. I devoured television, magazines, movies, and treasured books. There was a joke in the family that when I was a baby, I loved to eat newsprint. The message behind that story is that I reached for and stuffed tiny pieces of newspaper in my mouth because even as a baby I loved feasting on words.

I was born into a world where in some parts of the country, there remained signs marked "Colored" and "White," but I spent my childhood growing up on streets in Washington, DC's Columbia Heights neighborhood where Black and White lived together.

Harvard Street was lined with two and three-story Victorian houses with steep gabled roofs and round towers. They were beautiful houses, formal and inviting. I was born into a black-and-white world, but I saw everyone on Harvard Street; elderly White ladies with blue-tinted hair sat in front of their apartment building on high-backed benches during the summer evenings in flowing flowered print dresses and white heels. Black people with government jobs had bought houses on the block.

I would not know until I had published many books of my own that Jean Toomer, the great writer of the Harlem Renaissance, had been raised at 1422 Harvard Street five decades before I raced past the house where he was born to the nearby corner store to buy candy.

We lived at 1450 Harvard Street, my mother, father and I occupying the first floor. The first floor stretched from my parents' large bedroom at the front of the house, which had a wide picture window that looked out onto the street, to a living room with an upright piano, a large gilt-framed mirror on the wall, and a red and green Oriental carpet. The dining room was open and airy. My bedroom was tucked behind the kitchen.

My sister was ten years older than me and had married young. She sometimes came to visit. On the second and third floors were the "boarders" who rented a room from my parents to live in, along with the right to use the kitchen for cooking. The people we shared 1450 Harvard Street with were nurses, construction workers, and bus drivers who worked hard but couldn't afford to pay for apartments. They were the most interesting people I knew, their lives filled with as much drama as the characters in the books I read. The more they told me about their lives, the more I wanted to know.

Sometimes, when I was bored, I'd quietly pad along the hallways on the second and third floors, hold my breath, and press my ear against the closed or locked doors behind which the boarders lived their lives. I wanted to know everything. What it was like to be a grown-up, what it was like to be a woman, what it was like to be a man. I didn't know it then, but I was already a writer. I was doing what writers did— asking questions, imagining worlds that didn't yet exist, and finding solace in my own company.

I had lots of friends, loved racing the boys on the street to see who could get to the corner first (I usually won), and played Monopoly on the back porch in the summer with the kids next door. I felt most myself, however, in the attic, a small room with a slanted ceiling under the roof. I turned it into a retreat where I wrote in my diary and read my books. I placed a blanket there for my visits and pillows on the floor. Gazing at me as I read or wrote or slept were pictures from *Life* and *Look* magazines, striking black-and-white photographs of Dr. Martin Luther King Jr., preaching from the pulpit of his church or leading a civil rights demonstration, and a color photograph of Jackie, the beautiful wife of President John F. Kennedy.

In the attic, I learned that being alone is not a bad thing, and that alone, I was growing into myself. When I grew older and began to write articles, essays, and books, I would conclude that time alone writing, time alone thinking, time alone imagining was like saying a prayer. I would understand that 1450 Harvard Street was a laboratory where everything around me made me a writer.

It was at 1450 Harvard Street that my mother, Beatrice Lee Reid, anointed me. We stood at a table in the kitchen, both our hands coated with flour, kneading and shaping biscuits for dinner. Pausing the rhythmic kneading of the flour, her large hands resting on the mound of dough, my mother brought my eyes up to hers by her silence and her expectant breathing. When our eyes met, she said with stunning simplicity, "One day you're going to write a book." The words struck my ears like a foreign language. I had no idea what to do with such a monumental magic-laden statement. I heard it and I felt it as a weight I was not strong enough to carry. My mother, however, knew I could. As I realized many years later, that moment between us was a baptism.

My parents answered any question I had, no matter the topic, with honesty and a shake of their heads, amazed and pleased that my store of questions was inexhaustible. My father listened to me and my mother watched me. She watched me read anything and everything, from the leather-bound, red-trimmed *World Book Encyclopedias* my parents bought me on the installment plan to *Betty and Veronica* and *Superman* comics, two hundred of which were neatly stacked beside my bedroom door.

My mother watched and saw a girl whose love of books would inspire her to write books of her own. That is a vision that she could have held captive in her heart. Instead, she sent that vision forth and planted it in the soil of my latent fantasies and dreams.

My father once told me that when he met my mother, he thought she was the most beautiful woman he had ever met. My mother was stout and stylish, turning just the right hat or handbag from an accessory into a statement. She favored the reddest lipstick she could find for her full and slightly pouting lips, and her hair always gleamed from the application of Dixie Peach hair grease and the hot comb. She had come into the world to live a large life as a young woman leaving Greensboro, North Carolina, for Washington, DC. And by the time I was born, my mother had the house on Harvard Street.

When I rode with my father in his taxicab as he ferried passengers around the city, he urged me to see the wide world inside me. My mother pointed me toward the actual world, urging me to see all the places she had never seen and the countries she had never traveled to. I found stories about and pictures of the world my mother wanted me to see in the books at the Mount Pleasant Library several blocks from our house. After school, I'd change out of my school clothes and skate there.

Often, I heard adults talking about heaven. I listened as preachers described it. Always, it was portrayed as a faraway place somewhere in the sky, and you had to die to get there. I was still a child, but I knew what they didn't: that heaven was right here on earth, in the library.

With its broad columns and steep stairs leading to its double-doored entrance, the Mt. Pleasant Library resembled a church or a cathedral. I entered the library each time prepared to honor the rule to be silent even as my explorations filled me with curiosity and joy. There was the reading room with a fireplace and round tables and plenty of wood chairs with spindle backs. I became an explorer in the library on an expedition whose destination I could not predict. My pleasure was increased because I had no idea what world the books on the shelves would next reveal. My search for stories was random, leading me to choose a book because I found the face of the author on the back of the book jacket haunting and unforgettable, or because the story was set in one of the countries my mother told me she wanted me to visit. The musty smell of books, as though they were lives that had been fully lived, nourished my hunger for what I did not know. If I opened a book to a page where a reader had scribbled a note or a question, the sight of those words whetted my appetite to join the conversation.

I'd wander into the Adult Books Room, finding the volumes there more strange and therefore more enticing.

I didn't always understand what I was reading, but I had learned that words and sentences had many meanings, and that kept me reading to try to decipher what to my young eyes appeared to be a puzzle.

I was drawn to big, thick books that by their size and length promised not just a read but a sojourn—*A Tale of Two Cities*, *Jane Eyre*, *Robinson Crusoe*—and by the time I was in high school, I had discovered one of the world's greatest writers, Leo Tolstoy, and read all 1,300 pages of his masterpiece, *War and Peace*. Then I read everything I could find about his life.

My parent's confidence in me allowed me to assume that I could and would be listened to and heard. I didn't just ask questions, I liked to let people know what I thought. And I thought a lot—about everything. A letter to the editor I wrote was published in the newspaper. When a fifth-grade teacher told the class that enslaved people were happy, I raised my hand, and when she called on me, I stood up and told the teacher and my class that my father had told me that the enslaved people were not happy and that they wanted to be free.

***

My parents always agreed about what they wanted for me. But more and more they couldn't agree that they loved each other, or that staying together was possible. When I was fourteen, after years of arguments and occasional physical altercations, my parents separated. Now 1450 Harvard Street was no longer home. My mother and I moved into an apartment in Foggy Bottom, near the State Department.

The first two years after my parents' separation, I was confused, sad, and often depressed. My mother was too. I saw my father infrequently and missed him every day. Who were my parents? Why had they shattered our family? Why couldn't they get along? They said they loved me, but it no longer seemed or felt that way. I cried at night in bed, muffling my sobs with my pillow. My anger and fear were justified, but I didn't want to burden my mother with dark, jumbled emotions that I was afraid even full expression could not change.

I told my diary everything I couldn't say to my parents or share with friends. The lined pages of the small book listened without judgment. The more I wrote on its pages, the more the book became my best friend in the world. I read more than ever, and sometimes the stories healed me. Over time, I witnessed the growth of a truce between my parents. I saw my father more often. He remained the father I loved and the father who loved me. Eventually, when he came to our apartment to give me my allowance and to hand my mother an envelope with cash, he'd stay for a while and sit at the kitchen table with my mother, where they talked and laughed like friends. I was happy at last, very happy about that.

* * *

Everywhere I looked I saw dramatic change. In November of 1963, President John F. Kennedy had been assassinated. His death became a period of reckoning for the country. The laws and rules of the black-and-white world were crumbling. The year before my parents separated, 250,000 people from all over the country gathered on the National Mall in

Washington to protest laws that made racial segregation legal and denied African Americans equal opportunity in jobs and housing, education, and voting.

Federal laws and practices made it extremely difficult for African Americans to borrow money from banks, to acquire housing in certain neighborhoods, and to vote without intimidation in state and federal elections throughout the South. All those people stood in the shadow of the US Capitol, the Washington Monument, and the Lincoln Memorial on August 28, 1964, and listened to civil rights activists proclaim that the time for change had come. There were many speeches delivered that day, but four words, "I Have a Dream," spoken by Dr. Martin Luther King Jr., were the ones the world chose to remember and to make iconic. A year later, the Civil Rights Act was passed by Congress, and in 1965, the Voting Rights Act outlawed states using racially discriminatory practices to prevent Blacks from voting.

At six o'clock each evening, the nightly news on TV was filled with footage of Freedom Riders riding segregated interstate buses, sitting where Blacks were not allowed to sit and being beaten by mobs of angry Whites. Students from Black colleges and their White student allies, sitting at lunch counters where Blacks could not be served, were harassed by Southern Whites. Those marching for justice, some as young as me, were mauled by German shepherds let loose on them by policemen, and the full force of water from firehoses propelled them down streets as they screamed in fury and fear.

I grew familiar with the faces of women like Rosa Parks, the most publicized Black woman to refuse to give up her seat on a bus for a White person in the South and be arrested for that act, and Fannie Lou Hamer, who rose from a sharecropper family to become an internationally known human rights activist. These women and scores of other men and women, White and Black, young and old, risked their lives for equality. As I watched them from afar, I learned the meaning of courage and even patriotism.

The new civil rights laws were a down payment on Dr. King's dream, a dream that had lived in the souls of Black Americans for hundreds of years. Many people felt that as a nation we were on the cusp of that dream coming true. That was all the adults around me talked about. My father respected Dr. King but cast his vote for Malcolm X, a member of the Nation of Islam who urged Black people to focus on building their communities and businesses and not seeking to integrate into the White world, which he likened to a house on fire. Malcolm X was a burning bush of a speaker, who before his murder in 1965 traveled all over Africa and the Middle East, meeting scholars, writers, and politicians of all races who inspired his evolution into a belief system of emphasized the shared humanity of all people.

Everything was being altered, adjusted, reformed. Witnessing this was part of my education too. Every new law, each challenge to the status quo blazed a new trail I would follow. The new laws meant that in Washington, DC, three thousand Black students could now attend newly integrated formerly all-White schools. I attended Western High School in Georgetown, one of DC's wealthiest enclaves. The building was imposing and serious and sat confidently atop a rise surrounded by a wide, meticulously landscaped lawn. The students were a mix of children of ambassadors, diplomats, and the city's political and economic elite, as well as Black middle and upper-class students from all over the city.

My English teacher, Miss Daughtridge, was a striking woman who wore a blonde bob and whose high heels clicked rhythmically as she walked the aisles of the classroom where she taught English. She was a demanding, provocative teacher who used the act of writing and reading to teach her students to think critically. I was precocious, often reading books and articles designed for adults. I had a large vocabulary and a broad set of interests. Miss Daughtridge, however, was not easily impressed and was the kind of teacher who was stinting with praise. But when she gave it, you knew you had earned it. She had the gift of the best teachers; when her gaze met yours, you knew you had been seen—you knew you had been understood. She encouraged me, and I was willing to revise and rewrite again and again to earn a coveted A from her. Writing for the school paper, I met Wanda, who became my ally and sister-friend as we journeyed into adulthood.

Working for the student newspaper as a reporter, I made friends and discovered a community of other students who found a thrill in working with words. We covered class elections, building improvements, student clubs, and school fundraisers, but as we lounged in the newspaper office after school, we talked about older siblings who had been drafted to serve in the war in Vietnam, considered what colleges we wanted to attend, wondered if we dared to march or protest or get arrested for a cause, and wondered who had tickets to see Stevie Wonder at the Howard Theater or who was having a party at their house that weekend.

***

And then the world as we had known it was extinguished on the night of April 4, 1968, when Dr. Martin Luther King Jr. was assassinated in Memphis, Tennessee. Five years after the optimism of the 1963 March on Washington, Dr. King had gone to Memphis, Tennessee, to support a sanitation workers' strike. He was shot and killed as he stood on the balcony of the Lorraine Motel.

If a young person today researches that historical moment, they will find statistics about the days that followed—riots in over a hundred cities, thirty-nine people killed, and 3,500 people injured nationwide. Black communities across the country suffered property damage that would take decades to repair. In Washington, DC— the U Street Corridor where I'd gone to movies and visited on alternate Saturday mornings to get my hair washed and curled, over nine hundred businesses were damaged over four days of unrest.

For my friends and I, the shock and grief was immeasurable. A man who had devoted his life and his message to peace and nonviolence had been brazenly murdered while on a mission to foster economic justice. This is how it happened:

> The assassin James Earl Ray, already in Memphis staying at the New Rebel Motel, discovers that Bessie Brewer's Rooming

House is adjacent to the Lorraine Motel. He decides to change his location and checks in to Bessie Brewer's.

3:30 p.m.: Ray rents Room 8 under the name "John Willard," but asks to change to Room 5B, which overlooks the Lorraine Hotel. Ray discovers that the bathroom window has the best direct line of sight to room 306 at the Lorraine.

4 p.m.: Ray purchases a pair of binoculars at the York Arms Company for $41.55 and returns to his room at Bessie Brewer's to watch for King.

5:55 p.m.: Dr. Martin Luther King Jr. and Reverend Ralph Abernathy exit their hotel rooms after changing for dinner. The two, plus others on King's staff, are to attend dinner at the home of a local minister, Reverend Billy Kyles. Emerging out of his room, King lingers on the balcony to talk to his driver, Solomon Jones, in the courtyard below.

6:01 p.m.: Martin Luther King was shot and wounded badly.

Source: *American Experience*, PBS

My friends and I felt the anger of those both inconsolable and irrational in their grieving who took to the streets. We wanted to riot but didn't. We cried as we talked on the phone for hours. The fires, smoke, burning, and mayhem that were being televised unfolding on the streets bubbled instead in our hearts.

Back at school, we were dazed and sought comfort in group hugs and long quiet talks about what this meant for the world and our place in it. We felt betrayed by a country that our parents had taught us to honor despite its failings. Whatever had remained of our youth seemed to be dissolving fast as we thought about summer jobs and colleges in the fall. The death of Dr. King released a long-overdue flood of money and opportunities for young people like me and my friends at Western, young, gifted, and Black students who had been prepared by their families to be ready to walk through the doors of equality when White society finally decided to open them after generations of protest, activism and legal challenges to segregation.

Two months after the assassination of Dr. King, Senator Robert F. Kennedy, the brother of President John F. Kennedy and then a presidential candidate, was assassinated as well. These back-to-back killings convinced me and many others that America had rotted at its core.

CHAPTER TWO

Pride, Power, Passion— The Tree of Knowledge

I entered American University in the fall of 1968 as one of eighteen Black students chosen from DC public schools to receive Frederick Douglass Scholarships that covered our tuition room and board. We had graduated high school as Negroes and entered American University as Black people. We were angry and anguished but had a sense of purpose and mission imposed by what the murder of Dr. King had told us about America. Our idealism was a distant memory. Black Power and Black Pride activists like Stokely Carmichael and H. Rap Brown revised the meaning of Black, a designation that for generations among many Black people was considered a curse. Now it was an affirmation and an assertion.

AU is nestled in the prosperous neighborhood of Spring Valley, a wealthy, largely White enclave that I had not known existed before my entrance to American University. As I rode the bus to my classes up Massachusetts Avenue, past Embassy Row, where over a hundred foreign embassies were clustered, past Ward Circle and the sprawling green lawns and imposing homes, I knew I was entering a world that had never expected my entry. The Black domestic workers riding the bus with me to jobs cleaning the houses we passed gazed at me with pride as I clutched my books and copy of the *New York Times.* My mother had given me a subscription to the *Times* when I turned eighteen.

We had written a new dictionary defining ourselves and our world. There was Black pride—James Brown sang "I'm Black and I'm Proud," which we made an anthem, Nina Simone's "Young, Gifted and Black" became an anthem—and, in the lines of the poets Nikki Giovanni, Don Lee (who would become Haki R. Madhubuti and would found Third World Press), Mari Evans, and Gwendolyn Brooks, there was Black love—both Black self-love and Black love of one another.

We were Black, not Negro. We were victims of oppression, not racism. The response to the death of Dr. Martin Luther King Jr. was not riots but rebellions. At American University, there were the books I read for my classes in English, American studies, philosophy, and biology, and then there was a different kind of required reading as I pored over books about global Black life, history, and culture not included on the class reading lists. If the Mt. Pleasant Library was heaven, American University was nirvana.

In the aftermath of the cataclysms of the spring of 1968, publishers rereleased books by Carter G. Woodson *(The Miseducation of the Negro),* Lerone Bennett (*The History of the Negro*), and John Hope Franklin (*From Slavery to Freedom*). Much of the work of W.E.B. DuBois became available, along with books by John Henrik Clarke, J.A.

Rogers, Vincent Harding, and others. These historians and their prodigious body of work had been marginalized and sometimes erased. I devoured those books.

I spent hours in the library researching, writing papers, and, as I had when younger, exploring the stacks, stumbling upon knowledge, and in that way, power. Within a decade after I left American University, the works of Black women writers Toni Morrison, Maya Angelou, and Alice Walker would be required reading in literature classes at many colleges and universities. In the early 1970s, these women were at the beginning of what would become illustrious careers. I read their books and saw myself on every page.

My professors were passionate about the subjects they taught. White, mostly male, and mostly politically liberal, many were sympathetic to the growing militancy of the young Black students they found themselves teaching, and I was mentored by several of them. Professor Charles Larson, who had served in the Peace Corps in Nigeria, returned to the US with a love of African literature. He made it his academic specialty, and I took every course he offered. We developed a decades-long friendship. Larson became an important scholar of African and African American literature, writing essays and articles and authoring groundbreaking books that expanded and enhanced the field. Years later, he would ask me to write an introduction to a book he edited, *An Intimation of Things Distant: The Collected Fiction of Nella Larsen*, one of the Harlem Renaissance's finest women writers.

Professor Frank Turaj taught American literature with enthusiasm and unabashed love of the subject. Professor

Charles Hardwick made the subjects of philosophy and religion both mysterious and irresistible. When I became a teacher many years later, I worked to infuse my teaching style with the best of their influences.

The only Black professor I had in my four years at American University was Professor Theodore Hudson, a professor of English at Howard University who taught part-time at AU. Hudson expertly guided us through the deep and wide canon of African American literature. He was the quintessential gentleman and scholar. As much as I appreciated my White professors, I and the other Black students were elated that Hudson was available to us even part-time. Like us, he had lived the literature we were reading.

It mattered who stood at the head of the class as an expert, teacher, or mentor. The issue was about much more than symbolism. We needed more Black faculty at AU as a matter of equity and as a way of showcasing the brilliance of Black intellectuals and their contributions. Everyone on campus from students to faculty to administrators needed to see Black scholars at work.

American University's Black Student Union, known as OASATAU (the Organization of African and Afro-American Students at the American University), applied pressure on university administrators to spearhead the hiring of Black faculty and administrators and worked with them to accomplish this change.

We cocooned ourselves in Black identity, finding it a medicine that healed a generations-old ailment. I made this journey with my best friend Wanda, who I'd met at Western High School. We stopped straightening our hair and wore our hair natural. We sat in the Soul Corner of the cafeteria with the other Black students. We dated the African students studying International Affairs. We discovered jazz and the works of Black visual artists. Now we knew that we could be *Black and Proud,* and we tried to be that 24/7. We were brazen, bold, Black. Riding the bus to campus, I'd read the *Washington Post* and see front-page photos of sunglasses-wearing leather-jacketed Black students sitting-in on the floors of the offices of university presidents, sometimes with rifles and shotguns, demanding Black studies programs.

I'd never regularly been in the midst of so many White people, and I was often the only Black student in my classes. My fellow White students had often attended all-White schools, and thanks to what America had done to us, we looked upon one another as alien and strange although we were citizens of the same country.

* * *

I was writing furiously militant poetry with titles like "Exceptional Nigger," a poem that contrasted my status as a student at a respected White university with the plight of other Black people, the ones mired in life in the ghetto, which we now called the Black community. There were so many Black people crippled by untreated trauma, redlining, urban renewal, job discrimination, pay disparities, people whose families had been locked in turmoil as a result of systemic racism. I looked like someone who had made it "out." I was the kind of young Black person who made it easy for White people to say, "You are doing well, why can't other Blacks be like you?" All the books I was reading informed me why.

I was also writing poetry about love, family, and pride. My poetry was published in two anthologies, one edited by Nikki Giovanni entitled *And Night Comes Softly* and *Today's Negro Voices: An Anthology by Young Negro Poets*, compiled by Beatrice M. Murphy. I joined the staff of the *Eagle*, the campus newspaper. I was developing a critical consciousness that would be the foundation of my writing in the future. All the books I read that echoed my father's stories, along with all the classroom discussions of history and literature and science, instilled in me an awareness of how indispensable words were in shaping personal, political, and national identity. I wanted to continue to complete and complicate the story of Black people, Black women, Black children, and Black men. I would use words to bring discomfort where it was needed to rouse the sleeping. I'd use words to apply a balm where healing was required. I had no idea as a nineteen-year-old sophomore at American University that I was unconsciously shaping that manifesto, but I was.

In the fall of 1969, a year and a half after Dr. Martin Luther King Jr.'s assassination, Washington still bore the scars of the "uprising," as we called it, that had been a dramatic act of grief and grieving in the city's Black neighborhoods. This was my city, and I often walked past the cavernous remains of burned, scorched, hulking buildings, piles of rubbish, and empty lots on 7th Street and 14th Street NW. I was a poet, and I was also a journalist, and so I brought both sensibilities to a long photo essay. "Home...Where the Soul Is" covered four pages of the October 24, 1969, issue of the *Eagle*.

I wrote about what was gone and what remained, about the people who still called those streets home. I wrote about the prostitutes still on the corner, the men still waiting for something outside of liquor stores, and the men philosophizing in the barber's chair.

In the aftermath of the destructive response to the murder of Dr. King, Afrocentric and politically militant, community-oriented groups were created in cities all over the country. Along DC's U Street corridor, there was Pride, Inc., founded by future DC Mayor Marion Barry, his then-wife Mary Treadwell, and community activist Rufus "Catfish" Mayfield. I sometimes volunteered with the organization, which trained young people for various jobs and worked with ex-offenders as they transitioned back into the community. American University accepted students applying for admission to the university through Pride, Inc., which came to be one of Barry's many springboards into political power as it made a positive impact on the lives of hundreds of young people in the city.

In the essay, there were sections titled, "Of Black People Waiting," "After the Fires Were Out," "Building Better Ghettos," "Liberating Addicts," and "Out of the Ashes." I concluded the essay:

> There are two kinds of businesses on 14th Street now, those that are Black owned, and those that are owned by whites but have Black people "fronting"—acting as manager and owner (all in preparation for the fires next time). The former are usually record stores

with low prices, dwindling sales, and few customers, or wig shops that sell natural wigs, ranging in colors from black to pink to brown.

And on the streets...every other space is a vacant lot, some still filled with last April's rubbish, increasing the feeling of emptiness that still permeates these streets. Posters advertising the Soul Children or reading "Black Socialism, Pathway to Real Capitalism, Buy Negro Bonds" decorate boarded-up windows and stores. Laundromats and liquor stores with names like Afro Brother Liquors or Soul Bro. Liquors average two to a block. At 14th and Euclid, a black mural stares at you. It's one of the many painted after last April, vivid live colors clothe the drab red bricks, and images of Ron Karenga and a Black woman and child dominate the colorful scenes of Black life. Somehow the wall seems to symbolize a new spirit that has risen from the ashes surrounding us still...it's in the smiles of street corner men as they greet you as you walk past them with "hello sister," or a brother in a passing car suddenly giving you the fist... it's in the new sense of something we have that goes deeper than just pride. And the test of this new sense about us will come in our ability to sweep away these ashes that remain

and build something real, something lasting,
something all our very own.

I was given freedom to write whatever I wanted for the *Eagle*,
from a review of the latest album by Ike and Tina Turner to
reviews of novels or poetry by new Black writers. I enjoyed
writing my biweekly column until the column in which I
called out Black Panther leader Eldridge Cleaver for a speech
on campus; during this speech, Cleaver had been blatantly
sexist and substituted the words "power to the pussy" for
"power to the people" as he urged Black women to withhold
sexual favors from Black men until they "got it together."

The phrase was a crude allusion to the classical Greek
play *Lysistrata*, in which Greek women deny their men sex
until they negotiate peace during the Peloponnesian War.
Cleaver wanted Black women to deny sex to Black men until
they were ready to become Black Panthers. I remember
cringing in anger at the bawdy laughter that roiled through
the crowded auditorium, filled to standing room only with
Black and White students. Cleaver made the declaration with
the solemnity of a political theorist or a cleric announcing
a divinely inspired edict. In my column the following
week, I criticized Cleaver as more of a sexist showman than
a revolutionary.

My criticism did not sit well with the local chapter of the
Panther organization. In the lingo of the time, when dealing
with critics, the Panthers "didn't play." I had not known until
later that the female editor of Howard University's campus
paper, the *Hilltop*, was "visited" by local Panthers after she
wrote a piece questioning Panther tactics and ideology. It was

a visit that I heard involved threats of physical retaliation, although she was not harmed.

After the column was published, for several weeks, sunglasses and black beret and leather-jacketed members of the Black Panther Party regularly appeared on campus. They headed straight to the Soul Corner, asking the Black students studying, playing bid whist, or relaxing where I could be found. I had been warned by several friends on campus that "The Panthers are looking for you," so I only attended classes and put in my twenty hours a week at my work-study job doing clerical work in the dean's office. I went "underground" as much as possible. Everyone rallied for my protection and offered the Panthers not a single lead about how or where to find me. Taking a stand and criticizing the powerful and the popular could come with a cost. I watched my back but was determined to keep writing. This, I assumed, was the price of the ticket.

In my junior year, my mother suffered a cerebral hemorrhage, and then died after six months in a coma. For years, her health had been growing increasingly fragile. She had high blood pressure and painful arthritis, walked with a cane, was overweight, and had begun showing signs of dementia.

During the months my mother lay hospitalized in a coma, I soldiered on, attending classes, writing, and visiting my mother, stoically going through the motions of a life that had been capsized by trauma and grief. I was distant from my father and my sister for different reasons, and they were shell-shocked as well. My mother had been a linchpin ensuring the continuance of our erratic bonds. Who would we be, I wondered, if she died?

Each academic success I achieved had strengthened my mother's pride in me and her resolve to live to see me fulfill what she saw as my enormous potential. My philosophy professor, Charles Hardwick, suggested that I might like to transfer from American University to Antioch, a respected liberal arts college in Yellow Springs, Ohio, a change which he could arrange, because he felt the rigor of its curriculum combined with the requirement that students engage in political and social activism would meet my intellectual needs better than AU. When Professor Hardwick proposed that I transfer, my mother urged me to take advantage of this offer.

But I couldn't imagine leaving my mother or Washington, DC. Her oft-repeated mantra was, "I just want to live to see you graduate from high school." That had become, "I just want to live to see you graduate from college." During those months when my mother lay in a coma and in the years afterward, I bundled my grief and stored it away, refusing to retrieve it. I had been raised like most young Black girls, to be strong, to bulldoze through obstacles and pain. I moved out of our apartment and went to live with my minister uncle and his family in Northeast DC.

My mother's death both broke me and gave me a mission. I had in my possession all the dreams she had given me, the inspiration of my father, and my raging ambitions. I wanted to write for my mother, for my father, for myself and for Black people. I had something to prove. I had someone to be. My mother had not lived long enough to witness that evolution, but I knew she remained watchful and saw me wherever she was.

Because my mother remained in my mind, omniscient and ever-present, she walked across the stage at Constitution Hall with me as I accepted my diploma when I graduated from AU. She rushed into my father's arms with me as I ran toward him after the program. We had begun repairing the breach between us, and I was held aloft by our imperfect, indestructible love.

By the time I graduated from American University, I wanted to study journalism. I had dated a young Black journalist whom Professor Larson had introduced me to. He was a feature writer for the *National Observer*, a popular weekly national newspaper, and he often told me, "I get paid to be curious." I loved that idea: getting paid to be curious. I'd been curious since my days of listening to the conversations behind closed doors of the boarders at 1450 Harvard Street. My creative writing talent and promise had been confirmed by Nikki Giovanni, then called the "Princess of Black Poetry." My professors routinely gave me As for my papers, and the students who read what I wrote for the *Eagle* had become fans. Journalism would take me into the wide world, where my mother had always wanted me to be. Reporters covering the Vietnam War and the Civil Rights Movement changed history, like the men and women my father had told me were my ancestors. My mother was still watching. My father was too, and so I applied to Columbia University's Graduate School of Journalism, considered the country's top school for journalists.

CHAPTER THREE

Biting the Big Apple

The application to Columbia required six essays that I wrote over several days. The quality and nature of the questions were so rigorous that it was clear that the application process was designed to weed out the unfocused, the faint of heart, or those easily intimidated. I was none of those things. Still, on the first day of classes, when the dean informed the hundred entering students that we had been accepted from a pool of 1,200 applicants, many of whom were seasoned journalists, I felt a mixture of pride and awe at my good fortune. However, months earlier, when I received my acceptance letter, I had faced a moral dilemma.

I was offered a five-thousand-dollar scholarship which would cover the three-thousand-dollar tuition for the year-long program and leave me with two thousand dollars for living expenses. The scholarship was underwritten by Gulf Oil, an energy company that in 1972 was engaged in activities that supported the forces of racism and colonialism in the war-torn African nation of Angola. I took world affairs and politics seriously, and I was in anguish over taking what was essentially "guilt money" set aside for Black students by a company sapping economic and political opportunity from an African nation. After several days of thinking long and hard about who I was and who I wanted to be, and sharing my concerns with my best friend Wanda, I decided to take the scholarship and dedicate myself to writing, speaking, and possibly teaching in ways that made me "an intellectual provocateur." That way, I reasoned, in the future I envisioned for myself, I could be a counterforce against the greed and avarice of multinational companies like Gulf Oil.

Still, the day I read the acceptance letter from Columbia was the first time I had felt joy since the death of my mother eight months earlier. I went on to attend graduate school in New York City, while my best friend Wanda attended New York University's Theater School. Wanda had performed in several local productions of plays by Black playwrights while attending AU. My father's satisfaction in this accomplishment was muted. He knew how hard I had worked. He was proud of me but had long wanted me to go to law school and wasn't convinced that either my journalism or my poetry would pay the bills.

In Manhattan, Wanda and I lived in a tiny apartment on the Upper West Side between Columbus and Amsterdam Avenue. It was an apartment with a bathtub in the kitchen, which was not unusual as we discovered in our search for housing, since many of the city's apartments were often pieced together from separate and previously unconnected rooms, broom closets, and kitchens.

We had made this audacious journey together from Washington, DC, a black-and-white city, to a city of technicolor, insomnia, bright lights, and skyscrapers, and we loved it immediately. The first night in our apartment, we walked fifty blocks from our apartment on 92nd Street to the heart of Broadway at 42nd Street. We walked on that cool late August night past bodegas (corner stores); restaurants offering Cuban/Chinese cuisine; palm readers; Korean grocers, their fruits and vegetables overflowing from crates; expensive boutiques; bookstores; head shops; Lincoln Center; subway stations every few blocks; and people, all rushing past us. People avoiding eye contact, people walking dogs, people buying papers and magazines from a newsstand on every corner: this was just Manhattan. There were four other boroughs we had yet to see. One was Queens, the most ethnically diverse county in the country. Everything was amazing.

Most of my time was spent on the Columbia campus on Morningside Heights, a neighborhood located in Harlem. Columbia instilled in us the belief that we were the best and the brightest, that we were future leaders whose mission was to uphold a long tradition of journalistic excellence. *So, this is how the ruling class remains the ruling class*, I would often think ruefully in this rarified environment. I was part of a small but diverse contingent of Black students and other students of color entering in the fall of 1972.

From day one, my classmates and I were thrown into the intense news mix of the city and covered the same stories professional reporters wrote about for the *New York Times* or that aired on the local news stations: a demonstration at the United Nations, a political rally in the Bronx, a city council hearing, or a mayoral press conference. We had deadlines to meet and three times a week produced a newspaper. There were classes in journalistic theory and practice, but the most important thing Columbia gave me was confidence. I was challenged, tested, expected to perform, and expected to produce. I knew that Ernest Hemingway had started as a reporter before writing his novels. Instinctively I began to realize that the research and interview techniques I was learning, along with the comfort I had begun to feel looking at a blank page because I knew that I could fill it, were preparing me for anything and everything else I would write.

At Columbia, I finally got to work closely with and be mentored by Black faculty. An internship at the *Baltimore Sun* the summer before I entered Columbia had soured me on covering crime and hard news beat deadlines. I was drawn to feature stories and long-form journalism that allowed me to dig deeply into an issue or personality. My advisors were Phyl Garland, a seasoned journalist and the New York editor for *Ebony* magazine, who became the first Black female tenured professor of the "J" School, and Luther P. Jackson, who had preceded her as the first Black professor hired by the department. Phyl was earthy, low-key, and laughed easily; Luther was more reserved and scholarly. From both, I learned about the history and groundbreaking work of the Black press and how Black newspapers and magazines had traditionally covered whole swaths of American history left uncovered by mainstream media. They read my stories and gave me solid critiques.

Up to then, I had been fortunate to have been mentored by many talented teachers. However, Phyl and Luther provided advice on dealing with issues of racism, as well as how to navigate a career in White-controlled spaces. They offered invaluable support and inspiration to me and the other Black students.

During that year at Columbia, I wrote articles for the *Amsterdam News*, the Harlem-based newspaper founded in 1909 that remained one of the country's most important Black papers. W.E.B. DuBois had written for the *Amsterdam News,* as had Harlem's representative in Congress, Adam Clayton Powell. The paper was the first to publish articles by Malcolm X. I wrote feature stories and covered arts and entertainment, contributing articles for free just to list the prestigious outlet on my resume and add to the clippings of my published work that would later convince magazines that I had professional experience. Writing those articles provided me with a "byline"—my name beneath the headline.

In New York City, I was living in the center of the Black arts universe. Some were calling this fervent explosion of Black artistic and intellectual activity the Second Harlem Renaissance. Wanda and I attended book signings and readings at the Frederick Douglass Creative Arts Center Fred Hudson had founded. I was published in the pages of *Black Creation*, a literary journal that was the voice and the soul of young Black writers who wanted to write and to be heard.

Toni Morrison was then an editor at Random House on Manhattan's East Side, where she had been appointed the first Black woman to be a senior fiction editor. In that role, she would convince political activist Angela Davis to write a memoir and edit the fiction of Toni Cade Bambara. The searing, soaring plays of Amiri Baraka (formerly LeRoi Jones) were must-see events that we regularly attended. There were poetry readings by June Jordan and Audre Lorde at Louis Michaux's African National Bookstore on 125th Street. Michaux's, as it was called, was considered a temple of Black books. The store was on the same corner from which Malcolm X had enthralled Harlem's residents with his bold, revelatory attacks on American racism.

Jordan and Lorde were respected and revered for the beauty of their poetry and their political activism. After their readings at Michaux's, on different nights, I timidly approached each woman and thrust sheaves of typed copies of my poems into their hands and asked if they would read them. Without hesitation, they agreed to look at them. Both poets encouraged me to continue to write and told me that my poetry showed promise.

June Jordan was an award-winning poet with a growing audience as well as a feminist and a trenchant commentator on global and national politics and race. She became known as "The Poet of the People" when in 1991, while on the faculty at the University of California at Berkeley, she founded the Poetry for the People arts/activism project, which trained her students to take poetry out of the hallowed halls of academia into schools and community organizations, working with teens and young adults. The program still exists.

I will always remember the evening I lay on my bed reading a magazine and answered the phone to hear the voice of Audre Lorde on the other end, telling me that she had read my poems and thought I had talent and should continue to write. By the time I hung up from the call, I was nearly levitating with joy and satisfaction.

Audre Lorde was a fiercely brave and passionate activist and writer who spoke boldly on feminism, lesbianism, and race. She wrote that "women are powerful and dangerous" and called herself a warrior poet. She would chronicle her fourteen-year battle with cancer in *The Cancer Journals* at a time when open discussions of the disease were taboo. In 1981 Lorde and fellow writers Cherrie Moraga and Barbara Smith founded Kitchen Table: Women of Color Press, which was dedicated to furthering the writings of Black feminists.

My professors at American University modeled exceptional teaching. At Columbia, along with my other professors, Phyl Garland and Luther Jackson prepared me for the honorable yet often unappreciated work of the journalist. Audre Lorde and June Jordan and a nationwide cadre of Black writers modeled literary activism as a crucial element of a writer's life. I was mentored and shaped by some of the most important writers, intellectuals, and activists reimagining and recreating the world's cultural landscape.

***

I was "young, gifted and Black," and I was everywhere all over the city. Snapshots:

The scene: a Saturday night party on the fourteenth floor of a West Side apartment. Wanda and I are "getting down" with a group of South Africans studying in the US or living as exiles in the US because of their resistance to that country's apartheid regime. We have friends from all over the world and define ourselves as intrepid voyagers through a city of eight million people that attracts dreamers like us from everywhere.

Donny Hathaway's soulful groove "The Ghetto" is blasting, his voice a croon, a moan, the synthesizer that announces the song raising the room's temperature. No one parties with the fervor of our brothers and sisters from the African continent, and I am on the dance floor, in this moment insanely happy, dancing to this music. I am dancing to "The Ghetto" with famed South African trumpeter Hugh Masekela, an exile from his country and an international star, whose recording of the song "Grazing in the Grass" was topping the music charts and selling millions of copies worldwide. At this moment, Masekela and I are movin' and groovin' and finger snapping, joyously riding the wave of Donny Hathaway's voice and instrumentals, working up a sweat like everyone around us.

* * *

Wanda and I are sitting at a small table in a cavernous dimly lit club in Brooklyn, where jazz saxophonist Pharoah Sanders has made his instrument wail and cry for an hour. Sanders had played with John Coltrane and was known for blasting harmonic sheets of sound that made him in the estimation of Ornette Coleman, another musical great and fellow saxophonist, "the best saxophone player in the world."

The sounds of his instrument seemed to capture all the fury, pride, power, and anger in the air at that moment. Shirley Chisholm had become the first Black woman elected to Congress, having run a Presidential campaign that was met with virulent racism and sexism from all sides. Nonetheless, she became an inspiring and iconic figure. Richard Nixon was then president and was pressing on with a war in Vietnam that had become a daily carnage. I was a feminist and a Pan-Africanist and was seeing myself more and more as both a citizen of America and of the world—the world of many languages and cultures and religions, the world that my mother had said belonged to me.

After Sanders' set, I went backstage and quietly introduced myself. Sanders had eyes that pierced and a stillness that was frightening and impressive. I had asked Wanda to go backstage with me to steady my nerves. In my mind at that moment, I was nobody. He was somebody, and I was going to ask if I could interview him for a profile for *Black Creation*.

When I finally nervously whispered the request, he smiled in a flicker and said he knew the magazine and he'd be glad to talk to me. That is how I found myself a week later sitting in the Brooklyn living room of Pharoah Sanders.

* * *

During my second semester at Columbia, my father died of a heart attack. His death came a year and a half after my mother's passing. In the days and weeks after his death, I trembled as I wondered how I would have felt had we not worked, not just to repair our relationship, but to build a new one. During my visits home during the holidays and long phone calls, my father and I engaged in conversations that were intimate and honest, conversations that I came to cherish.

No longer was I the little girl entranced by his tales of larger-than-life heroes. I yearned for my father to tell me the story of who he was, who he had been, and what his life had meant. He did. We were bound by stories until the end.

* * *

Despite my frenzied consumption of all New York had to offer and the writing opportunities I found on my path to making my name and writing my way into the world, I remained grief-stricken. I had not processed in any formal way with a minister, counselor, or therapist how much I missed my mother and how angry I was about her death.

Each accomplishment felt like a sadistic piercing of my soul because my mother, who was so deeply invested in my success and achievements, had not lived to witness the life I was living, the life I was creating using her ambitious blueprint.

My father's death made me in my mind officially an orphan. And despite the pride and esteem my parents had nurtured in me, during the time when I was despairing and searching for an answer to why they had both died within two years, I subconsciously concluded that my parents' deaths confirmed that I had not truly deserved their love. If they had loved me they could not and would not have deserted me. If they had loved me, they would have lived to see me become the writer they had made me. That convoluted, dangerous conclusion was never spoken openly even as it bubbled constantly in the depths of my mind.

For nearly a decade, this dark story was a source of my drive, even as it crippled me as I sought to find and fashion loving relationships with men. In time, I would heal with the help of a talented therapist and my thirst to find a way to be happy. Still, the dual departures of my parents, both too soon in my eyes, also meant that in everything I wrote, I was writing to my mother and father, writing for my mother and father, trying to honor them and bring them back to me.

My parents had lovingly ordained everything I had done since entering college, everything I had done since coming to New York. My father's stories of African glory and achievement paved the way for me to become friends with African students, eagerly pumping them for information about their nations I would never read in the *New York Times*. My mother told me again and again, "Get some education and no one can take it away from you." And so, I educated myself not just with books, but also with questions, quests, and people. My mother had left Greensboro, North Carolina, for Washington, DC, stepping into her own broader horizon. I was already planning to travel one day to some African nation, joining the hundreds of Black people making the pilgrimage.

My father wanted me to become a lawyer instead of a writer. But lawyers *are* writers. They are storytellers, shaping narratives about guilt, innocence, culpability, and liability for judges and juries. Years later, I would write books about the lives of Black women and Black families that readers would tell me changed their perspective, gave them courage, or allowed them to find personal freedom. The words I would write could be as impactful as a lawyer's summation or a sentence handed down by a judge.

After I graduated from Columbia, rather than apply for jobs at newspapers or TV stations, I chose to try my hand at freelance writing. In the 1970s, magazines thrived, were widely read, and were (along with newspapers) as influential as today's social media and internet. I wanted to write articles for magazines because I loved having an extended deadline to investigate, interview, and come to conclusions about a subject. I had not yet written for a major magazine, but I had my eye on one magazine in particular. The first copy of *Essence* magazine was released in 1970. The magazine featured beautiful Black women of all hues on its covers, and inside, investigative articles about topics of interest to Black women, from politics to culture and lifestyle. Its initial circulation of 50,000 copies a month grew to 1.6 million. Famed Black photographer Gordon Parks was the editorial director during the first three years. The magazine became a symbol of Black beauty and style; if you were a Black woman, you read it, and if you were a Black writer, you wanted to be published on its pages.

My day job was as an editorial assistant in the publicity department of Doubleday Publishing Company, which a decade later would publish my first book. I learned how the publishing industry worked, writing press releases and handling media and administrative tasks for the director of the children's books division. I was grateful to leave it all behind at five o'clock and spend my evenings researching and interviewing for articles.

I requested and was granted a meeting with the assignments editor of *Essence*; my degree from Columbia, as well as the stack of feature articles I had written for small journals and papers, convinced her to take a chance on me. My first assignment was to write a piece examining the issue of Black feminism, a subject that had inspired a cultural guerilla war among Black male and female scholars, writers, activists, and policymakers.

Black feminists like Florynce Kennedy and Eleanor Holmes Norton called out the White feminist movement for focusing on the lives of middle and upper-middle-class White women while excluding dialogues with women of color that included the recognition of the history of racism as a factor in the lives of Black women along with sexism. The upper-class White women, who were eager to begin fulfilling careers and who were the primary audience of organizations like the National Organization of Women (NOW), depended on the underpaid and often exploited domestic labor of African, Caribbean, and African American women as nannies and housekeepers to make their dreams come true.

Although the National Black Feminist Organization was founded in 1973, many in the Black community argued that, for Black women, the issue of racism was central, and that aligning in any way with "feminists" derailed Black political progress. I was assigned to write an article capturing the vigor, diversity, and substance of Black women's views on the topic. I interviewed Black women politicians, activists, and scholars, including Toni Morrison, who had published *The Bluest Eye* and was recognized as powerful novelist with a unique voice, a trenchant observer of society and politics, and a scholar of Black history and life.

I trailed behind Morrison as we entered an elegant French restaurant a few blocks from her office at Random House, where she was greeted by the maître d' and the waitstaff with the kind of respect and officiousness usually reserved for monarchs. Morrison schooled me on the topic of intersectionality.

In an interview a decade later published in *Conversations with Toni Morrison*, she said, "One doesn't have to make a choice between whether to dance or cook—do both. And if *we* can't do it, then it can't be done!" The interview for *Essence* was the first of two interviews I would eventually conduct with Morrison, the second years later at a literary festival. Both times she struck me as a woman of depth who had found her voice and knew how to use it.

The confidence she radiated, which felt nearly steely at times, originated in a family that nurtured her gifts. She told me she grew up hearing ghost stories from her parents and how that shaped her imagination. Her family house was set on fire by the landlord when she was two. She attended Howard University and later taught there. She was divorced, raising two sons as a single mother while trailblazing as a Black woman in corporate America and creating a sisterhood of Black women writers, some of whom she published. What I learned from Morrison in that interview for *Essence* was that "of course, I am a feminist," and that Black women, whether they acknowledged it or not, were inherently feminist.

As I worked with the *Essence* editor, I struggled to learn how to insert my point of view, narrative, meaning, and texture into these long features. While the interviews provided information, I had to provide the reader with context and narration in my own voice and from my perspective that allowed them to access the full meaning of the story. After several drafts, I became comfortable with becoming "part of the story," and so I could acknowledge that I was a feminist, which in some parts of the Black community was heretical.

The article was published and generated letters to the editor, praise, and buzz. I made $1,500 and was so excited I took a photograph of the check, framed it, and put it on my bedroom wall. I already knew that I was going to write my way to Africa. The money I made writing would fund my trip.

My next story for *Essence* dealt with another issue that had been uncloseted: rape. Women lawyers, feminist activists, and legislators were working to eliminate rules of corroboration and evidence that made rape convictions difficult to win.

Rape was a controversial topic in the Black community because, for generations, enslaved women had experienced rape as a frequent and normalized part of their victimization. After Emancipation, White men used rape as a terror tactic against Black women, a crime for which they rarely, if ever, were prosecuted, while Black men were routinely falsely accused of raping White women and paid for the "offense" with their lives. And yet Black women were raped most often by Black men, and like many rape victims, frequently chose not to report the violation for fear of not being believed or of being humiliated in court, or more ominously, fearing they could be accused of inviting their sexual assault. I was assigned to examine these bedrock beliefs and fears in my article.

These realities convinced me that few women would be willing to talk about being victims of sexual violence. Yet once I began informing women in my circle of friends about this assignment, dozens of women contacted me, eager to share their stories. Eager, because they had never told anyone. Eager, because they wanted to release the sense of shame they carried. Eager, because they hoped their stories would initiate change.

In addition, my editor told me that it was important in this piece to profile victims and victimizers. What, she wanted to know, turned a man into a rapist? My research revealed that a prison in New Jersey had developed a special psychological treatment plan for men serving time for rape and sexual assault. I spoke with the director and asked if I could interview some of the men in the program.

The day I entered the New Jersey prison and walked past the men in their cells, my head wrapped in African cloth (a galae) and clutching my tape recorder and notepad, as I walked by, I heard the whispers: "*Essence* is here. *Essence* is here." I interviewed three African American men who were serving sentences ranging from six to ten years. Each man had benefitted from the therapy sessions and intensive program designed to heal them. As a result, they spoke with insight about who they had been, what they had done, and why and who they were becoming.

Jake, tall and light-skinned with reddish brown hair, told me that that as a child he had been brutalized by his mother, beaten with an ironing cord, and locked for hours and days in the bedroom closet. Monroe, greying and wearing horn-rimmed glasses, recalled being raped repeatedly by his older uncle and being told that he would be killed if he told anyone. All the men I spoke with shared histories of being victims of sexual and/or physical violence, of living with untreated trauma, of walking through their lives unsuccessfully trying to tamp down and dissolve the rage that had been planted in them. When the rage exploded, they raped.

Jake told me that he was serving time for raping a woman on the campus of Rutgers University, where he had worked in the cafeteria. "It was late at night; I was headed to where I could catch the bus, and I saw a young woman coming out of the library. I saw her, but I didn't see her as a person. I felt suddenly overcome with anger and rage. It was like I was in the grip of a flashback to all the feelings of pain my mother had inflicted on me. I didn't even feel like me. It was me, I'm not trying to say it wasn't, but when I began following her and pushed her into some bushes behind the library and raped her, in that moment, I didn't feel that pain that was always there; I felt powerful, I felt like I was somebody. It took making her invisible for me to feel real even for just a moment."

As I rode the bus back to Manhattan, I quietly wept for those men and for the women they had violated. Writing that story radically altered my concept of crime and criminality, victims and victimizers. I was growing in confidence and ambition. After two years at Doubleday and the success of my freelancing, I was ready to work in media and was hired as an associate producer at the local PBS station in New York. I worked on a nightly talk show that featured interviews with newsworthy writers, filmmakers, politicians, and scholars.

I was pleased with my freelancing success, but I now wanted to expand the range of stories I wrote. I wanted to write more than feature stories based on the real world. I wanted to use my imagination; I wanted to write fiction. I wanted to write stories only I could create. I asked other writers where I could take evening classes in fiction, and they suggested the New School for Social Research, located in Manhattan's East Village. That's where I took an introductory fiction workshop with Sidney Offit, who had written several successful novels for young people.

Affable, warm, and an excellent teacher, Sidney encouraged me and saw in my highly autobiographical short stories both imagination and skill. He called me one Sunday morning with effusive praise, telling me that I was "the greatest thing since sliced bread," an old-fashioned expression that nonetheless convinced me that I could write more than just journalism. We went on to develop a long and satisfying friendship.

Offit's belief in me was a talisman I held close. His encouragement echoed the support of my parents. Offit joined a circle of mentors who gave me the strength to meet the world head-on. All these mentors made me a writer. I think that people need encouragement to write not only when they show great promise, but even when, and perhaps because, they don't. No other endeavor has revealed to me more about what I am capable of and who I am. Writing is too important to be left only to those who love it and can't live without it. We all have a right to write. And we all deserve to be taught how to write well. What we write is a form of instruction to the world, where the first seeds of the dreams we hope to harvest are sown.

And yet if encouragement is crucial, writers also need humility as they approach the task of learning to write well. Encouragement gets you started and keeps you writing. But one of my most important lessons about how to become a good writer was rendered by a writing instructor who didn't believe I had "the right stuff" at all. Buoyed by Sidney's support and praise, I followed his advice and enrolled in a fiction writing class offered by another teacher at the New School for Social Research. Sidney's classes were often a joy to behold and experience as he critiqued our work, joked, teased us, and told great stories about the famous writers he knew. His rigor was so thoroughly camouflaged by an avuncular personality that most students initially had no idea just how much we were learning or how much we were being challenged, although the results showed up in successive drafts of our stories. We just loved Sidney, and he made mastering the art of writing seem possible with hard work and diligence.

The new teacher was a woman of late middle age whose dour visage looked out on the assembled students in her class like a vicar searching for signs of heresy. The unease and tension that many years later I was to find permeating the atmosphere of so many writer's workshops in MFA graduate programs was the air we all breathed in that classroom. We were in boot camp, and we were looking at the drill sergeant. Naturally, or rather as luck would have it, my story was the very first one read and "workshopped." I am grateful that my memory has erased many of the details of this traumatic experience. But I vividly recall that not only did the teacher not like the story, but she found not a single redeeming virtue in the piece, not a line worth salvaging. I recall the pitying shakes of her head as she discussed the story, as though wondering how anyone could imagine such a travesty, and then having imagined it, could commit it to paper. The critique seemed to last the entire hour and a half of the allotted time for the class, but of course it did not.

The other students in the class gazed at me nervously as she discussed the story, and my hand trembled as I reached for it when it was passed back to me. Somehow, I sat through the remainder of the class, but once we were dismissed, I hurried from the room, wiping away tears. Humiliated and confused, the next day I dropped the course. The intervening years have allowed me to turn this anecdote into a tale of youthful vanity that I share with students in my writing classes.

I've come to call her style of critique the Pol Pot School of Criticism, after the leader of the Khmer Rouge in Cambodia in the mid-seventies, who imposed years of death and destruction on the people of that nation. Many renowned teachers of writing believe that an emerging writer's ego has to be broken down and rebuilt. But like all of the most dire forms of political reeducation, this process is more about destruction than creation. The most miserable, confused writers I have met, who often grow to hate writing, and in the process themselves, are victims of this faulty pedagogy. I've met scores of talented writers derailed for years by criticism that was much more about the teacher's need to be a dominant force in the lives of their students than about working with and building on a writer's strengths. If not for a deep well of emotional resilience and years of encouragement, that teacher's words might have convinced me to stop writing completely.

The teacher seemed heartless, but in the most dramatic way possible, she introduced me to the other side of the writer's life. No writer can receive unanimous praise from everyone all the time, nor should they expect such universal accolades. If encouragement is necessary to keep writing, making peace with criticism of one's work and the necessity for criticism is just as important. After I dried my tears, I comforted myself with the explanation that the teacher was cruel, clearly misguided (for hadn't Sidney liked my stories?), and an awful teacher. But the real lesson she taught me, albeit with all the finesse of Attila the Hun, is that while criticism hurts (all the time, no matter how many books you've written), it is inevitable and crucial for artistic growth.

If I had allowed myself a few days or a week or so to get over my hurt feelings, it is quite likely that I could have seen more than a little value in the teacher's words about the story. Sometimes as a writer you have to "kill your babies"—that is, simply chuck a piece of writing that has won your heart, and dispose of a story that you are besotted by. In other words, if it is broken, we have to fix it. But we have to be able to see that it's broken to fix it. Perhaps I didn't need to reject all of that teacher's judgment.

My agent and my editors are professional skeptics who are difficult to impress, all in the service of forcing me to become a better writer each time I begin a project. Tough questions, interrogation of intent, and the proposing of alternative approaches all puncture the armor we writers encase ourselves in, an armor made up almost entirely of ego. Criticism *can* give us new ideas about our work and challenge us to justify the choices we have made. Still, as much as I learned about developing a thick skin from my second fiction teacher, I learned much more about the craft of writing and what I *could* do as a writer from the first.

***

The memoir *Migrations of the Heart* is the book I wrote to try to understand my life and turn that life into literature. It is a memoir that is multilayered and sprawling. It is the story of growing up with my father's stories and my mother's faith, of coming of age against the backdrop of the civil rights and Black Power movements, of falling in love with a Nigerian graduate student, making a life with him in Nigeria, giving birth to my son and myself, and returning to America.

The story of how I came to write a memoir at the age of thirty is an informative odyssey that illustrates how writers are claimed by stories and how publishers decide what to print. While at Columbia, I met and fell in love with Femi, a Nigerian graduate student. For several years, Femi became my safe harbor. He was a supremely confident architectural student who wore his confidence, his pride in his roots, and his plans for his future as easily as a second skin. As I stumbled through heartless grief, he was a balm for my battered soul. Wrapped in the embrace of the large Nigerian community Femi was part of, I no longer felt abandoned. I loved him. And I desperately needed him to rescue me from the turbulent waters I secretly sometimes felt myself drowning in. His love for me, my love for him: I was convinced that our life together would bring me back to shore.

After my father died, I moved in with Femi, and we lived together in his Brooklyn apartment, where after the emotional impact of my father's death I felt grounded and at peace. When Femi returned to Nigeria, I followed a few months later. The city of Lagos, where we settled, was the capital of a country with the largest population in Africa. The nation had survived the brutal Biafara War, during which the eastern regions had attempted to secede. Revenue from newly discovered offshore oil reserves filled the nation's coffers. Yet corruption on all levels was rampant. I witnessed and lived through what happened during and after a military coup. And yet Lagos pulsed with a bravado, drive, and pride that had made it a cultural capital of the continent. Nigeria was the home of writers Chinua Achebe, Wole Soyinka, and the Afro-beat master musician Fela Kuti. The country was an economic powerhouse and Nigerians—as thinkers, inventors, migrants, and scholars—held outsized influence everywhere. If you wanted to know Africa, you had to know Nigeria.

Only the strong survived the capital city of Lagos, with its hydra-headed "Go-Slow" traffic jams that were a testament to and by-product of the infusion of money, construction, foreigners, and rapid change. A hard-charging city, the communities ran the gamut from Ikoyi, the equivalent of New York's Upper East Side, where the wealthy and powerful lived behind gates guarded by night watchmen, to much of the rest of the city, where families lived in tin shacks, where determined young men and women rose each morning and left those shacks dressed in white shirts and ties and pressed pants, or in Western-style skirts and heels, to find or create their "Nigerian dream." We lived in Surulere, one of the many "suburban" communities ringing Lagos where middle-class Nigerians, teachers, lawyers, doctors, and successful market women lived in houses that promised electricity and a steady water supply.

I was mentored by an African American woman from Oklahoma who was married to a gentle, easy-going accountant on how to survive as an American woman in a culture and country that I found both seductive because I felt an ancestral/racial kinship and maddening because I was constantly reminded that I had not really "come home."

Turmoil, challenge, and change were the hallmarks of the four years I lived in Nigeria, where I taught in the mass communications department of the country's major university, the University of Lagos. Within a year of my arrival, I suffered a miscarriage; a year later, I gave birth to a healthy baby boy that we named Akintunde ("the spirit of the father returns"). I continued to write articles for *Essence*, including one on the challenges of cross-cultural marriages. A group of Nigerian journalists wanted to launch a Nigerian women's magazine inspired by *Essence* and sought my advice.

And as I had in the US, I woke at four o'clock five days a week, meditated, performed thirty minutes of yoga, and worked on a novel that had "possessed" me for several years. My professional horizons expanded, even as with each passing year, I felt the walls of my union with Femi closing in and threatening to crumble.

One summer when I made what had become an annual trip back to the States to visit family and friends, I met with Marcia Ann Gillespie, the editor of *Essence*, and told her that I was ready to show the novel to an agent. She recommended I contact Carol Mann, who had just opened a literary agency on Manhattan's East Side. I had no idea the day I walked up the winding stairs to Carol's tiny office that we would become friends and that she would be my agent for the next forty years, and remains so to this day.

I had sent Carol the manuscript of the novel, and we met to discuss her thoughts about the book. She was brown-haired, with an open, eager gaze. We talked for a while about her company, and then she told me that she was impressed with my writing but not so certain about the novel. Then she quickly inquired, almost breathlessly, "So tell me about your life in Nigeria." Carol folded her hands on her desk and shifted slightly as though to get more comfortable in her chair.

No one, not family members nor friends, had ever asked me that question with the optimistic expectation I heard in Carol's voice. When I talked with friends about living in a country where my Blackness was the norm and how I no longer felt the literal and figurative burden of racism, I saw in their faces partial acceptance of my words.

Yet I knew that my friends and family had read and seen accounts of coups and the stories of famine and poverty on the continent. I knew that more than a few of my family members thought I'd lost my mind, choosing to live in what I knew some of them saw as "the heart of darkness."

My feelings about living in Nigeria were complex. I loved the sight of the women of Nigeria, whose skin color and body shape echoed my own. There was a palpable sense that by living on the African continent in one of the continents' most influential nations, my life and its meaning were highly charged. I'd constructed and held to an identity wedded to Africa and Africans. Corruption was rampant in Nigeria, as was tribalism. But wasn't American racism corrupt?

Didn't American capitalism turn the American Dream into a nightmare for many? Wasn't the progress African Americans made, whether political, social, or economic, perennially met with White backlash? I wanted my son to grow up in an environment where he could feel the intense pride in who he was that his father felt, not threatened by racial profiling or self-doubt because of the color of his skin.

Carol was an agent. Her job was to look for great stories, to find them and encourage writers to tell them. She was not convinced that at that moment, my novel was the great story I had to tell. So I told her about my life in Nigeria, living as a highly educated feminist in a deeply patriarchal society that still circumcised female babies, where there was no concept of a "single woman" since a woman's value was entirely related to marriage and motherhood. I described my husband's family, how his father had had twelve wives and how some of my husband's family members practiced polygamy, and my journalism students, who were smart and ambitious and hungered to improve their country and to visit America. I recounted to her the tremendous creative and intellectual energy I had witnessed in so many Nigerians, from women selling meat in the market to boys hawking fruit on the side of the road to my colleagues at the university, and the twixt and tween lives of Black women married to Nigerians who struggled to honor themselves and who they were as well as the culture they were now a part of. Many of us were feminists, and we had shared with one another our fears of raising girl children in our adopted home.

When I finished telling Carol about my life, I felt as though I had met myself for the first time. "Why aren't you writing about that?" she asked gently. I had been so busy living that dramatic, conflict-filled, and compelling story that I had never assessed it. It was mine to live, not mine to dissect and reimagine, which is what writing requires.

"I want to write the novel. Not about my life," I told her with a slightly defensive insistence.

"All right," she said. "But that's the story you should write. Please, let's stay in touch."

I left her office elated and confused. Carol thought I was a good writer, and she wanted to stay in touch with me. But she wanted me to write a story that, as I found myself on the sweltering sidewalk outside of her building, I had no idea how to compose and did not want to construct. I'd have to confront the increasing fissures in my marriage, the emotional incompatibility with Femi, the nagging cultural differences I could no longer ignore, and how as that marriage was spiraling toward dissolution, no one in his family would or could understand my growing anguish and the fear that if I walked away from our union, I would lose my son.

* * *

When I returned to Nigeria, I knew my life there was over. Slowly, day by day, I dreamed of a new existence, I saw my experience as Carol Mann had, realizing that my life contained the elements of a compelling narrative. At the age of twenty-four, I had followed my heart and my hopes to another country, became part of a polygamous African family, and became a university professor and mother, all while grappling with the pressures of cultural differences and the weight of my unaddressed grief. To the people around me, I was the same woman as before. What was invisible to their eyes was how I had been transformed. Now I was possessed by the lure of writing a complex, dimensional narrative. *A narrative about me.* I'd feel this possession many times in the years to come. It is a feeling at once sublime and utterly peaceful. Its hold feels like both a grip and an embrace. Possessed, I have been given a creative mission that feels imperative and that I don't fully understand yet don't question. Ironically, I had wanted to write a story that only I could imagine. I thought that story would be a novel; instead, it was a memoir. Only in the writing of *Migrations of the Heart* did I realize how much of our lives we imagine and how much they rival the most satisfying fiction.

For a writer, a story branded with their name on it is irresistible and seductive. It is an invitation for which there is only one possible response. I felt myself, my body, my soul, working on an elevated plane. On that level, I made a binding commitment to write my story. I did not know how to write it. But writing is perpetual problem-solving, and so I knew I would figure that out.

As I was strategizing about both how to leave my marriage and how to write about it, I became a researcher, interviewing Femi's family members for details of Yoruba culture and life that I would need for the book. Any information about Nigeria, the country, and its people that in my four years there I had taken for granted or overlooked I now revisited. With new, more observant eyes, I looked at faces closely, assessed personal interactions between people everywhere, and turned Femi's older brother into an anthropologist who educated me about the customs and beliefs of the family I had become a part of.

I was a vulture circling over the impending ruins of my life—a vulture riddled with sorrow, guilt, and regret. Writing would turn an experience that threatened to live in my memory only as ashes into material that could resurrect and redefine love, hope, optimism, and joy, all the emotions I'd initially felt when Femi and I met, emotions that despite the dark days, had been real.

I'd written poetry and journalism that I was proud of and completed a draft of a novel that I'd been told didn't quite make the grade. I knew what a well-crafted book could do. Powerful, beautiful stories had given me life all my life. That's what I swore I would do for myself and my readers.

CHAPTER FOUR

Coming Home

When I returned to the States, I was a single mother teaching at a community college in the Roxbury area of Boston and was still grieving the separation from Femi even as I realized there had been no other recourse. As I accepted the mantle of writer and potential author, I was reborn again. I thought a lot about what I wanted to write and how I would present myself to the world. I decided to use my middle name, Marita, as my first name. My mother had named me Bernette in homage to her brother, my uncle Bernard; Marita was my middle name. But at this point in my life, I wanted to name myself. Marita had always been positioned after my first name and before my last with a tantalizing energy. Marita. I fell in love with my middle name and claimed it now as my first name, the name I would hold and carry and the name that I felt was perfect for the writer I was becoming.

I presented Carol with a sixty-page proposal for the book I envisioned. She subsequently submitted it to Marie Brown, a Black editor at Doubleday, the same publishing company where I had worked as an editorial assistant eight years earlier. When Wanda and I arrived in New York years before, she introduced me to Marie, whom she had met through a professor at NYU. That sunny afternoon in

Marie's small corner office, Wanda and I chatted with her about our adjustment to the city. I had no idea then the role that Marie would play in my life. Marie was at that time one of only a handful of Black editors working at trade publishing companies in New York. In a decades-long career, Marie Brown, working as an editor and then an agent, became a midwife to a whole generation of Black writers whom she represented, befriended, advised, and mentored. While Marie loved the book proposal, a year passed before she offered me a contract—a year in which she had to sell her fellow editors on the book and ensure that Doubleday was not considering any competing titles so that when she presented the book at an editorial meeting, she could count on the support needed for her to offer me a deal.

Many of Marie's fellow editors had never heard of or read *Ebony* or *Jet*, Black magazines that had been mainstays in the Black community for generations. Some didn't even know about *Essence*. They were White liberals who lived their lives for the most part hermetically sealed against any meaningful knowledge of Black people and Black life. When it came to Black folk, despite their love of literature and the arts and their dedication to books and reading, most of these editors had massive blind spots about Black people. No matter how talented the Black writer or how salable their book idea was, Black authors faced an uphill battle in the editorial boardrooms of most of New York's publishing houses in the 1980s, publishers with workforces that were 99 percent White. But Marie, who had successfully published several bestsellers by White authors, won the battle for *Migrations of the Heart*.

Published in 1983, fourteen years after *I Know Why the Caged Bird Sings* by Maya Angelou but before a veritable tidal wave of memoirs by women writers turned the genre from niche to respected literature, *Migrations of the Heart* was the book I had to write so that I could write everything that followed.

As I learned how to write the book, learning with each word and every sentence, learning by excavating memory and unleashing imagination, I was terrified and elated. I was terrified to tell the story and risk censure, criticism, judgment, and bad reviews, yet elated by the prospect of fulfilling my mother's prophecy that I was destined to one day write a book. To conquer my intense fear of exposure, throughout the year I spent writing the book, I played a curious but effective psychological trick, convincing myself that I was writing a novel, not a memoir. This wasn't *my* story I was writing, I told myself, but the story of a "character" named Marita. This mental mind game relieved the anxiety that sometimes threatened to derail my progress.

One evening, in frustration I browsed through the pages of the memoirs of Langston Hughes and Zora Neale Hurston, praying silently that on their pages I would find the code to write my story. Whatever techniques I studied in their memoirs, I had to find my way word by word into my narrative. I used all the training and experience I had as a writer, from poetry to fiction to journalism, because each genre had in different ways informed me how to write the book. The borders between genres were erected by publishers to sell books, not to liberate or buttress the creative process.

Writing *Migrations of the Heart*, I strove to create a world that resonated like a novel while writing from an open heart and an open wound, which is how a memoir reads and feels. I decided to write about coming of age as the world changed in unprecedented ways and as women and people of color were claiming and asserting their rights. I wrote for young people who could use the book as a social document that captured a social and historical moment that I knew was important. I wrote to be read in the future.

On publication day, I stood in a downtown Boston mall and saw copies of *Migrations of the Heart* prominently displayed in the window of B. Dalton Books. I was overwhelmed with pride. Within a few years, *Migrations of the Heart* would be read in African American literature courses and would become required reading across campuses at universities nationwide. Scores of Black women would consider the book essential reading if they were involved in a relationship with an African, which inspired mixed emotions because I did not see my story as cautionary but as an inspiring adventure. The book was embraced by Black and White readers, and I began to learn the power of story to dismantle borders between people. For that alone I am proud to be a writer.

CHAPTER FIVE

Making It Real

I lived in Boston for five years, during which I first taught at Roxbury Community College, where my students were often first-generation African American college students or immigrants, working two jobs and taking part-time classes. I loved those students, most of whom were focused on succeeding and felt they had no time to waste. After two years, however, I was burned out by the heavy teaching load and needed more than the salary that forced me to teach part-time at other schools to make ends meet. I subsequently applied for a position in the English department of Emerson, a respected liberal arts college located in the heart of downtown across from the Boston Commons. With a higher salary, I moved from a small apartment in Mattapan to a spacious loft in the Piano Factory in the South End, a huge building as large as the US Capitol Building that provided working and living spaces for artists.

My love of Boston's wide variety of museums, institutions dedicated to arts and culture and education, and the fact that I had made friends with a mix of White, Black, and Hispanic singles and couples at a church I joined, were tempered by the city's virulent racism.

I experienced housing discrimination in my first year in the city when I called about an apartment and was asked about the origins of my name. When I applied for apartments outside of Black Roxbury and Dorchester, upon showing up, I was told the apartment was no longer available, which contradicted what I had been told on the phone. Some taxis refused to take me into Black neighborhoods. Within six months of moving to the city in 1979, I had written a front-page feature for the *Boston City Paper* about my experiences trying to settle in the city as a Black woman.

My application for an artists' loft in the Piano Factory coincided with the settlement of a class action suit filed by a group of Black artists who had charged the management with discrimination. South Boston was the province of the working-class Irish, and Blacks entered that territory rarely; when they did, they could face violence. When several young Black youths were chased out of the neighborhood by a gang of White teens and one of the Black boys was then hit by a subway train and paralyzed from the neck down, I knew that Boston was not a city where I wanted to raise my son.

After the publication of *Migrations of the Heart*, I began to realize that *I was a writer, and writing was what I was good at, what I loved, and what I would do for as long as I could.* Writing was my dream come true and my assignment from God, and I was ready to report for duty. That realization sparked in me a desire to live amongst a community of Black writers, a community that I had not found in Boston, but that I knew existed in Washington, then called Chocolate City.

* * *

So after several years teaching at Emerson, I went back home to DC, a city that I had associated for over a decade with the loss of my parents, a city that I thought of only with loss and grief. On my return from Nigeria, I could have chosen to settle with my son Michael in DC, but the wounds of loss still felt fresh. I remained traumatized and felt that to live in DC was to return to the scene of a crime that had scarred me and from which I would never recover. Yet now, here I was, coming home to where my father gave me indelible stories as a map and a gift and my mother gave me a throne that I was heir to.

Back home, I taught part-time in the English department of my alma mater, American University, worked with a local literary nonprofit, and wrote my first novel, *A Woman's Place,* the story of three young Black women who meet at a New England college and form a decades-long friendship.

In the years since the death of my parents, I had found and created family in friendships with women. In Nigeria, I was part of a small sisterhood of African American women married to Nigerians, women with whom I bonded, the friendships all the more intense because we often felt marginalized living in a culture that in some ways was in our bones but that remained impossible to decipher. Even in Boston, I formed "Sister circles" with Black women. Friendship with other Black women had been a major component of my mental health.

A Woman's Place is told in the shifting voices of three young women: Serena, a fiery political activist; Crystal, a moody, talented poet; and Faith, who is sheltered by her friendship with Serena and Crystal but drops out of Winthrop University where they meet and becomes a Muslim and marries a man many years her senior. Writing a novel is a test of so many things: imagination, patience, the ability to change course mid-stream, go where you don't want to go, and learn how to write regularly, as well as the ability to listen to the story and the characters. After I spent a year writing the first draft of the novel in third person, just as I wrote the last sentence, I realized that this was a story that required these young women to speak directly to the reader in their tender voices, voices that evolve over the years. So I rewrote a third-person novel in the first person. That's called just a day's work in the art and craft of writing. Doubleday had given me a two-book contract after *Migrations*, a sign of their faith in my future as a writer.

My first three books, the memoir *Migrations of the Heart* and the novels *A Woman's Place* and *Long Distance Life*, were all published in the 1980s. Courtney Thorsson, in her book *The Sisterhood: How a Network of Black Women Writers Changed American Culture*, tells the story of how Toni Morrison, Alice Walker, June Jordan, Ntozake Shange, journalists Margo Jefferson and Audrey Edwards, and other Black women writers formed a group named "The Sisterhood" to offer emotional and practical support to one another in their careers and their lives as Black women writers. Even more importantly, because many of the women were the *first* Black or woman of color trailblazers in media, publishing, and communications, they worked within their institutions to expand opportunities for other Black writers.

The Sisterhood was, however, just one block in the vibrant nationwide (and likely global) quilt of activism of

Black writers and publishing professionals. Wherever Black writers were publishing books, they were starting magazines and publishing houses. On the West Coast, Ishmael Reed was publishing poetry and novels and editing journals. Marie Brown published two groundbreaking anthologies by scholar Mary Helen Washington, *Black Eyed Susans: Classic Stories by and About Black Women* and *Invented Lives: Narratives of Black Women 1860–1960.*

Those anthologies, along with Toni Cade Bambara's *The Black Woman: An Anthology*, were foundational building blocks in the canon of African American literature that would be taught in the academy in the years that followed.

The decade of 1980–1990 witnessed the publication of seminal works by Black women writers whose scholarship, plays, essays, and novels like *The Color Purple*, *Beloved*, *Sassafras*, and *Cypress & Indigo* created a literal and figurative revolution in publishing. Black women writers critiqued Black male patriarchy, dared to expose the dark side of Black male and female relationships, and addressed mental health issues and domestic abuse.

By 1992, for the first time, three Black women writers had books on the *New York Times* bestseller list simultaneously: *Jazz* by Toni Morrison, *The Temple of My Familiar* by Alice Walker, and *Waiting to Exhale* by Terry McMillan. Black women writers did not just write books, they worked to change the industry that published them. I read the groundbreaking work of these women, was inspired and influenced by their work, argued with others about it, and realized that they had created a moment of lasting cultural significance. I owed my voice in some measure to them.

In DC, I found a thriving community of Black writers and became part of that community, which included Jonetta Barras, Kwame Alexander, E. Ethelbert Miller, (founder of the Afro-American Resource Center at Howard University), Patrice Gaines, Darrell Stover, children's book writers Sharon Bell Mathis and Eloise Greenfield, poets Brian Gilmore and Kenny Carroll, and many others. The most impactful connection I made on my return to Washington, besides Joe Murray, the man I would marry, was Clyde McElvene, who wasn't a writer but considered writers to be among the most important people a society produces.

I was interviewed about *Migrations of the Heart* one afternoon on *The Diane Rehm Show*, then a popular nationally syndicated program on the local NPR station, WAMU. Clyde heard the interview and contacted me. We met over coffee and talked for several hours. I had never met anyone who took books as seriously or understood their importance as he did, especially their importance for Black people, who had historically been jailed or killed for learning to read and write. Clyde told me that he was impressed by what I had shared in the interview and that he had ordered a copy of *Migrations of the Heart*.

He'd left a successful career working in marketing and promotion for a major record label to start his own consulting company working with small businesses and individuals on strategies to grow their companies. Clyde said the endemic corruption of the record industry had left him exhausted and cynical. He'd left the business to devote more time to working with Black people, especially Black youth, on issues of literacy, education, identity, and creating

Black institutions. With the passion of a cultural missionary, he had started and headed study groups around the DC/Maryland area devoted to reading classic works by African and African American authors. Over the next three decades, Clyde would become my "work husband" and someone from whom I learned something new every day.

Clyde favored dashikis and kufis, round brimless caps popular among men in the African American community as a sign of peace, renewal, or protection of the mind. He was a bibliophile who when we met had collected over 1,500 books by Black authors, a number that would eventually grow to 5,000. Clyde did not just handle books with care. He handled them with reverence and would talk about a new book by a Black author that he had discovered on one of his many forays to the library with the zeal of an explorer stumbling upon a new and irresistible world. I told Clyde that I wanted to form a local group to offer programs and support to the Black writers in the area. Before I could ask if he would work with me on that project, he asked "When do we get started?"

Clyde and I worked with other members of DC's Black writing community to form the African-American Writers Guild in 1986, which presented programs and conferences to benefit the local community of Black writers. We presented readings and invited nationally known Black writers to speak on everything from getting published to the writing life.

I joined the faculty of the MFA Creative Writing Program at George Mason University in Fairfax, Virginia, as an assistant professor; I taught fiction to the graduate students in the program, as well as writing and literature courses to undergraduates. I was experiencing career success with the publication of *Migrations of the Heart* and *A Woman's Place*. I also felt I was part of a Harlem Renaissance revival.

Terry McMillan burst onto the literary scene bringing a fresh, energetic voice and take on the lives of Black women. Alice Walker won a Pulitzer Prize for her novel *The Color Purple*. Toni Morrison had graced the cover of *Newsweek* upon the publication of her novel *Beloved*, and there were already whispers that one day she might win the Nobel Prize for Literature, which she did in 1993. Bebe Moore Campbell, Gloria Naylor, Pearl Cleage, Walter Mosley, Tina McElroy Ansa, Henry Louis Gates, Jill Nelson, Toi Derricotte, John Wideman, Octavia Butler, and so many others contributed to a fervent blossoming of Black narratives that transformed American culture. There had never been a more powerful moment to be a Black writer. We were writing in numerous genres, from romance to science fiction. Even more significantly, this generation of Black writers would leave a legacy of Black-founded and Black-led institutional support for Black writers that would endure.

I was part of that blossoming and wanted to recruit more Black students into the MFA program at George Mason. I also wanted to create an organization with a larger national profile than the African American Writers Guild.

Clyde and I filed the formal incorporation paperwork for the Zora Neale Hurston/Richard Wright Foundation in September of 1990. As a literary activist, I wanted to work in and on a larger cultural terrain. I named the foundation for Hurston and Wright because when I researched the writers, I discovered they had engaged in a long-running literary dispute that reminded me of the atmosphere during this golden age of Black writing. As I meditated about a possible organization, Black women writers faced virulent and often personal pushback, insults, and demeaning interpretations of their work that ran the gamut from critics on daytime TV shows like *The Phil Donahue Show* (which was then daytime's top-rated talk show until it was dethroned by Oprah Winfrey) to scholarly tomes from both Black male and some Black female writers and scholars. I learned that we had been here before, and because we had been here before, I felt the time was right for this organization.

From an essay by Henry Louis Gates, Jr., called "Why Richard Wright Hated Zora Neale Hurston" published in *The Root* on March 18, 2013:

> In an angry and suggestive essay on *Their Eyes Were Watching God*, Hurston's masterpiece, which reads more like an example of playing the dozens than a book review, Wright charged Hurston with pandering to the lurid tastes and fantasies of white males: Hurston's "prose," he says, "is cloaked in the facile sensuality that has dogged Negro expression since the days of Phillis Wheatley." Wright then accuses Hurston of "voluntarily continu[ing] in the novel the tradition which was forced upon the Negro in the theater, that is, the minstrel technique that makes 'the white folks' laugh."

In self-defense, she gave as good as she got: A year later, in a review of Wright's four interrelated novellas, *Uncle Tom's Children,* Hurston charged that Wright's novel wasn't concerned with "understanding and sympathy"; rather, it was "a book about hatreds," composed of "stories so grim that the Dismal Swamp of race hatred must be where they live." And the only role of sex in his book, she said, was as a motivation for murder: The "hero gets the white man most Negro men rail against—the white man who possesses a Negro woman." He gets several of them while choosing to die in a hurricane of bullets and fire because his woman has had a white man. There is lavish killing here, perhaps enough to satisfy all *male* black readers.

I knew that the name of this new organization was crucial. I wanted to signal that we were creating a space a place that honored both Black male and Black female writers. Hurston became my literary hero not only because of the beauty of *Their Eyes Were Watching God* but because she was a bona fide woman of letters, writing novels, short stories, plays, and works of journalism as well as revolutionizing the field of anthropology. We needed Wright's anguish and anger in *Black Boy* and *Native Son* as much as Hurston's humor, and unabashed love of Black folk, their lives and the lore they created.

writing workshop for Black writers, as inspiration for Voices of Our Nation, a multicultural summer workshop he helped to create. Each summer, Hurston/Wright Writers Week provided Black writers with a safe space within which to craft and imagine their stories. These were writers who often lacked a supportive community or who attended largely White MFA programs in which they felt their stories were too often misunderstood by fellow writers. They often found themselves the only Black writer in the room trying to translate Black existence to resistant audiences. Hurston/Wright Writers Week gave them confidence, mentoring, role models, community, and affirmation that their stories mattered. Open a book by a Black writer and you will likely see an acknowledgement of the role of the foundation in their lives and careers.

By the time I left George Mason and joined the MFA faculty at Virginia Commonwealth University, the Hurston/Wright college award was widely recognized. Virginia Commonwealth promised and provided financial support for both the college award and the Hurston/Wright Writers Week.

During a meeting held in an imposing boardroom at the Smithsonian Institute, where board member Steven Newsome worked in the institution's archives, board member E. Lynn Harris made a bold suggestion. With the college award established and respected and the summer workshop growing in popularity and attendance each year, it was time to do something new, something bold and exciting. E. Lynn suggested we introduce an annual literary award for Black writers. Hurston/Wright was then a decade old.

E. Lynn Harris was a big-hearted, life-loving, generous spirit who was one of the country's most commercially successful novelists and one of the foundation's biggest contributors. Openly and proudly gay, E. Lynn wrote depictions of African American men who were closeted or "on the down-low." Wildly popular with men and women, the novels were entertaining and regularly made it onto bestseller lists. E. Lynn had self-published his first book, *Invisible Life*; then, buoyed by the success of the endeavor, he quit his job selling computers for Hewlett-Packard and dove into the writing life. Now he, like me, was published by Doubleday.

E. Lynn was down-home sassy and funny and "roll up your sleeves, let's get this done." The board debated the idea of the annual literary award, with E. Lynn proposing an answer to every potential issue or problem raised. In 2021, the foundation presented the first Hurston/Wright Legacy Awards, honoring the global community of published Black writers in fiction, nonfiction, and poetry. The first Legacy Awards celebration was a formal dinner ceremony held at a downtown DC hotel. Congresswoman Eleanor Holmes Norton celebrated this new award, and Terry McMillan, by then author of *Waiting to Exhale*, which sold millions of copies and was made into a film starring Whitney Houston, spoke of the significance of the evening. Borders Books underwrote the Legacy Award for several years in the amount of $30,000 annually, with ten thousand dollars going to the winner in each category. The Legacy Awards dramatically impacted Black writers' lives and careers. Lynne Duke, author of the book *Mandela, Mobutu and Me*, told me that her publishers had not planned to issue the book in paperback. Several days after she was recognized with the Hurston/Wright Legacy Award she got a call that there would be a paperback edition.

With the enthusiastic support of writers, the publishing industry, individual donors, philanthropists, readers, and volunteers, we broke new ground. There was no other celebration like the Legacy Awards: Black writers honoring Black writers, with the recognition coming from their peers in a roomful of writers and readers whose presence solidified the enduring power of our narratives. In 2002, the Authors Guild presented me with their award for Distinguished Service to the Literary Community. Clyde and I had become channels to empower Black writers and honor their stories, as my father and my mother empowered me and seeded every story I wrote.

CHAPTER SIX

Witness, Witness

I was born into a family of ministers. My maternal grandfather, John Reid, was an unschooled part-time preacher in Greensboro, North Carolina. He was a silent, morose figure whom I only remember vaguely from annual summer visits to see my grandparents when I was a child. John Reid is chiseled into my memory as a tall, rangy, seventy-plus man, who instilled in me equal parts puzzlement and fear. I bonded with my grandmother, "Granny Reid," while helping her in the kitchen of a house that included a pantry stocked with shelves laden with jars of canned fruit and vegetables, produce picked from her backyard garden and orchard. Her kitchen was home to an ancient but still functioning squat and sturdy cast-iron stove. My grandfather, though, was mostly a presence to me, rather than a person, a presence who despite physical proximity seemed always elusive.

His oldest son, Bernard, one of my three uncles, had left Greensboro and settled in Washington, DC, following the migratory pattern of their only sister, my mother. In Washington, while my uncle Bernard was working in the federal government for many years, with his pay grade and levels of responsibility steadily rising, he followed in his father's footsteps and became a minister too. But my uncle, casting off the heritage of his unlettered father, went on to gain a divinity degree, to serve as an associate pastor for many years at one of Washington's oldest Black churches, and to found and head his own Baptist congregation.

One of my cousins is an elder in the Seventh Day Adventist denomination, and another is an associate pastor in the United Church of Christ. This familial impulse to serve as public witness to various forms of "higher truth" has marked me as well. My ministry is the written word. As a noun, "minister" means one who performs as the agent or instrument of another. As a verb, it means to give service, care, and aid. My uncle was, like his father, often silent, a man of apparently deep emotions that were conflicting and often misunderstood. Even before I was old enough to know much of anything about life and love, once I knew that my uncle was a minister, I suspected that he had become a man of the cloth in order to care for his own soul as much as the souls of others. That is why I became a writer. In most of my memories of my uncle, I see or define myself as distant from him, and yet in many ways we were kindred spirits.

During visits to my uncle and his family in their Northeast Washington home, I remember sometimes seeing my uncle sitting at his desk in his study, poring over the Bible, a Concordia, and the related texts that he used to develop his Sunday sermons. His study was a small room, more like a converted closet on the second floor of the house. There was a desk, a lamp, and a small bookcase. My uncle spent hundreds of hours in that small cell, reading and thinking about God. Clearly some of the most important moments of his life were spent in that room, where he discovered the message and the truth that he and his faith community needed to know. I only saw my uncle preach a couple of times. In the pulpit, he expressed everything that he was—serious, cerebral, a lover of language and words—and standing in the pulpit gazing out at his parishioners, he strove to be those things that I think he wished he was—humorous, passionate, and naturally at ease with himself and with others. Judgment came to my uncle easily and often. I am sure that too prompted him to preach. Yet he was generous, responsible, caring, and the solid rock in our family, a man whom in different ways we all depended upon.

I have often wondered what wounds, self-inflicted, inherited, or otherwise, my uncle sutured during those long sessions in his study. My minister cousin told me. "When you write a sermon, the first person you're talking to is yourself. If you want to know my business, what I'm going through, listen to my sermons." Even as a child I was in awe of my uncle's discipline, his steadfast willingness to cut himself off from the ebb and flow of family life and give himself over for hours on end to the Good Book, God, meditation, prayer, the eternally unknown that the believer convinces himself is or can be known. Like my uncle, I have been attempting to minister to my soul. I am always the first person, long before any reader, who needs the care found in the power of story and the written word.

As a Black woman writer, I write from the specifics of my experience in so many realms—as a woman, African American, American, daughter of my parents, sister, inheritor and creator of the life-altering cultural changes of a Black cultural movement, world citizen, mother, and wife—and I require all those designations, for each is the repository of a chapter from which my story springs. In that small study, my uncle wrote the religious good news for his parishioners, and the search for and articulation of the good news made his every day and every night worth living. A story can be an antidote, a gift, be it the story of a Messiah or a despised stepsister saved by a fairy godmother. My uncle and I mined different kinds of stories to create a larger space in the world. As a Baptist minister, my uncle was an intermediary acting on behalf of his parishioners in their quest to know and understand their God. Ministers are often asked when and how they got the call to preach. Family lore and gossip informed me that for my uncle, the call came during a crisis of confidence following a devastating divorce, a crisis that included an assessment of the life and lifestyle he had lived during that marriage. When the call comes, it often feels transcendent and absolutely perfect. My minister cousin told me, "When I graduated from college, I tried teaching and working in the government, but none of those careers fit. Then I started praying for guidance. God spoke to me through a sermon my pastor preached. The theme was 'A Call to True Discipleship.' The message was that we have to let go of what we're familiar with to honor God's calling in life and God will see us through. That's how I got the call."

I have spent my life responding to the urgent, frequent call to write. Writing that can ultimately transform the reader demands that I release preconceived notions of the story I have been summoned to tell. I have to let go of the familiar in order to honor and understand this sacred act that I have chosen and been assigned to perform. Just as my uncle's parishioners invested enormous trust in him as preacher, readers sign an invisible but binding contract with an author. The assumptions of a congregation and a readership are very similar. Both audiences expect their souls to be enlarged by hearing *the good news* embedded, encoded, sometimes even hidden in a *transformative* story, be it one grounded in myth, fact, imagination, or, as with most stories, a blessed comingling of all three.

* * *

The year was 1986, and Washington, DC, where I'd returned to live, like Philadelphia, New York, Atlanta, and Chicago was in the chokehold of a seemingly endless cycle of violence resulting from turf wars, "gang beefs," and generalized mayhem that accompanied the importation of crack cocaine and other drugs into Black communities. These were communities that had been defunded of investment in jobs, schools, decent housing, and youth recreation facilities. Instead, these neighborhoods were flooded with drugs, which became a commodity on which generations of Black youth bet their dreams, fantasies, and futures. We now know that the crack epidemic was a corrupt and nearly demonic outgrowth of historic racist engineering of the lives of African Americans. While it was happening, young Black males were labeled "an endangered species" as homicides in some cities, mostly of Black men, in some years of that awful epoch reached five hundred deaths annually.

Every morning I read another account in the *Washington Post* of Black males killed in "drug-related" acts of violence.

The names and the bodies were piled high in my mind and threatened to become dangerously anonymous. The question of who these young men were haunted me, and I imagined my way to an answer with my novel *Long Distance Life*.

I wanted to write a novel that would un-erase these young men, who in public perception were only criminals, purveyors of mayhem and violence. What were the forces that had made pushing drugs, despite the abbreviated lifespan that accompanied it, viable, attractive, and irresistible?

I embedded the story of two young men who had become ensnared in the city's drug trade in a story of six decades in the life of Naomi Johnson, a Black woman who migrates to Washington, DC, from Spring Hope, North Carolina. The life of my mother inspired the character of Naomi Johnson, and I gave my mother's literary alter ego her indomitable spirit and her passion for life and living.

To cover the 1920s to the 1980s in Black Washington, DC, I spent days in the Library of Congress. I was back in the library and loving every minute of it, as I had in elementary school and in college. I sat at the heavy wooden desks in the Thomas Jefferson Building Reading Room surrounded by a hallowed quiet as writers and scholars and the curious sat waiting for the books and microfilm and journals and newspapers we had requested to be delivered on carts whose wheels barely squeaked as they rolled from one patron to another. I pored over Black newspapers of the nineteen twenties and thirties for everything from advertisements for skin lighteners to an appearance by Duke Ellington at the Howard Theater.

I requested anything written that would transport me back to the days that would have witnessed Naomi Johnson's flight "up south," as Washington, DC, was called. I shared the story I was writing with older African Americans who in interviews informed me that at one time, DC had been home to scores of North Carolina and South Carolina Clubs where Black people who had migrated from hamlets and cities in those two states met regularly for emotional and material support. The children's book author Eloise Greenfield, who lived in Northeast DC, told me that in the nineteen forties, nearly all the Black people in her hometown of Parmele, North Carolina, had migrated to DC it seemed in the space of several weeks.

I interviewed scholars at the Smithsonian about the lives of tobacco farmers so I could convincingly create the life Naomi fled. Elizabeth Clark-Lewis, author of *Living In, Living Out: African American Domestics in Washington, DC, 1910–1940*, was an invaluable resource, sharing with me what led her to write her groundbreaking book about the lives of Black women domestic workers.

In *Long Distance Life*, my character Naomi attended a demonstration in front of the White House during the Roosevelt administration to protest the wrongful imprisonment of a group of Black men in a case that gained international notoriety, the Scottsboro Case. Naomi's fictional husband, Rayford Johnson, had worked in the Black Nationalist movement of Marcus Garvey, a movement that during the 1920s gained the allegiance of millions of African Americans and African-descended people all over the world.

Because my mother had inspired my creation of Naomi, I wanted to give Naomi what my mother had not experienced with my father: a deep, true, faithful, and satisfying love. I wanted to write a love story—a Black love story—at a time when so much of the literature Black women were producing was devoid of those kinds of narratives. Naomi's daughter Esther works in the civil rights movement. Esther's oldest son becomes a doctor, and her youngest son is a drug dealer. I constantly felt the literal and figurative soul of my mother as I wrote *Long Distance Life,* and there were moments when writing dialogue for Naomi felt as if I were transcribing my mother's words and thoughts.

This is a section of the novel inspired by my mother's spirit. She is narrating a crucial moment in her relationship with Rayford Logan, the man she marries.

Well, we'd been going together almost a year and I knew what I wanted. So one night he came to see me. I'd fixed pork chops, rice, gravy, collard greens and biscuits. He coulda took one look at that meal and knew I meant business. We listened to some Louis Armstrong records he'd brought over and then we got in the bed. Oh, he fixed me real good that night! And afterwards, we're lying there, him smoking them Chesterfield cigarettes he'd been smoking he told me once since he was sixteen, and I'm feeling all soft and warm and happy and I just asked him, just like that, to marry me. I hadn't never seen a man blush before, but Rayford laid there, looking like what I'd said had made his day.

When he got himself composed, he says, "You don't leave nothing to chance, do you, *Miss* Naomi Reeves?"

And I told him, "Only way I'm gonna get what I want is to ask for it. I always figure on hearing yes. And no don't scare me 'cause I heard no all my life and it ain't never stopped me. But smart as you are, I knew you'd have sense enough to say yes."

I created a moving love story, and I secretly wondered if it would be possible for me to experience what I had given Naomi in my imagination and prayed that it would.

After I submitted a near-final draft, I went to New York for a meeting with my editor, Loretta Barrett, a tall, imposing woman with a room-sized laugh, who, along with several other Doubleday editors, championed my work. She loved the novel but wondered why in the last third I chose to write a first-person narrative in the voice of Snookie, the hardened and hard-core drug dealer who seals the fate of Nathaniel, Naomi's grandson. That section was a shift from the point of view of Naomi, which dominates the book. "That section made me nervous," Loretta said with a slightly abashed smile. "Good, that's what I wanted," I told her. In the first-person narrative, Snookie tells his story, the story of his childhood, his more than drug dealer dreams, his anger, and his pain.

He tells the reader that he is much more than they think he is and that he wants to make a mark on a world designed to erase him. Loretta was asking me to defend that decision, to justify it. As a writer, I should be able to do that, and I was. Snookie remained in the book.

I was writing, and I was also working on myself very intentionally to move past emotional demons and baggage. I went back into therapy, and I also began a practice that I would utilize throughout my adult life of using affirmative thoughts to change my life. Reading Louise Hays' *You Can Change Your Life* changed my life.

Then, a year after the publication of *Long Distance Life*, I met *my* Rayford Johnson. His name was Joe Murray. I met Joe at a party. Joe Murray was a "race man" like Rayford, and like Rayford, he taught at Dunbar Senior High School. I love sharing this story. I made me a man! I dared to dream and wrote and believed my way to a happy ending through the novel (and through lots of work on *me*).

Long Distance Life garnered a glowing full-page review by Jonathan Yardley in the *Washington Post* Book World. Yardley was a major literary critic who mattered. He went on to name the book one of the best of 1989, and *Long Distance Life* spent a few weeks on the *Washington Post* bestseller list.

***

My son Michael was in middle school when one evening he asked me a question that would inspire my return to memoir writing in 1995 with *Saving Our Sons: Raising Black Children in a Turbulent World*. The question was, "Why would God let that happen?" My son was wrestling with grief in the aftermath of the loss of two friends, one a boy who was shot and killed at a party, the other, another boy who skipped school one day to join a group of friends and brought a gun to the meet-up. A few minutes later he was dead. Writing a book had become the way I attempted to answer the inexplicable, whether in fiction or nonfiction. And so my answer was to write.

Saving Our Sons grew out of an article I wrote for *Washingtonian Magazine* about the then-recent killing of Jay Bias, the younger brother of Len Bias, a college basketball player who had been signed by the Boston Celtics in 1986 and had died of a cocaine overdose, adding fuel to the passionate and often ill-informed national discussion of drugs and young people. Len and Jay's mother Lonise had become a sought-after spokesperson after Len's death, speaking about the dangerous journey American youth made from adolescence to adulthood, why drugs became a part of that journey, and what parents could do in response.

I used a format that I would come to call "communal memoir" as I narrated the story of raising Michael with Joe against the backdrop of systemic racism and urban violence. We were a middle-class family, and I told the story of a year in the life of a Black boy journeying into adolescence in a city with one of the nation's highest murder rates, a city in which homicide was the leading cause of death for young people his age. Nationwide, homicide was the number one cause of death for Black males. I interviewed sociologists, activists working with young Black males, and a young man once on the road to college who was in prison for armed robbery. I spoke with one of my most talented Black male writing students, and Michael's voice rings throughout the book as we journey to Nigeria to visit his father. I narrated the complexity of what it meant to be a Black male in America. I appeared on *The Oprah Winfrey Show*, and the book not only became a bestseller but was an important act of witnessing and testimony for me to make and take for my grieving community and city.

CHAPTER SEVEN

Teaching

While I was writing and working with Clyde on sustaining and growing the Hurston/Wright Foundation, I was also teaching. I loved teaching then and love teaching now. There have been four distinct phases of my teaching career: teaching writing as a faculty member of MFA or MA graduate creative writing programs at historically White universities, George Mason University, Virginia Commonwealth University, and Johns Hopkins University; teaching as a visiting professor and Distinguished Writer during visits to universities and colleges and working with a variety of diverse groups on campuses and in the community from youth to seniors; teaching Black writers in Hurston/Wright Writers Week workshops; and now working largely with Black women in what I call the University of Marita Golden (meaning my workshops in memoir, fiction, and publishing).

You can teach someone how to write. You cannot, however, teach someone how to live as though possessed—possessed by stories that call insistently for expression in written narrative. You can't teach someone how to have something to say. As a writer, I am haunted by themes that now live in the bloodstream of my imagination, and that have become the prism through which I meditate on the world. These subjects and themes shape the contours and create the fingerprints of the stories that I write.

Her name was Carly, and she was the fiercest, bravest, most beautiful writer I had worked with in several years of teaching in graduate creative writing MFA programs. I am sure that more than once, and on most days, the writing saved her—body and soul. She was not a diamond in the rough; rather, she was a gorgeous lily when I met her, a rare flower struggling to wrest itself from the poisonous grasp of the muck and mire that had somehow sprouted it.

By the time I joined the MFA faculty where I met Carly, there were about three hundred such programs at colleges and universities around the country. What an unabashedly optimistic idea, that one could enroll in a graduate program and learn to be a novelist or poet the way one learned to be a lawyer or a doctor. You could get a degree in creativity. Each year, the programs have grown in popularity. MFA creative writing programs generally attract late twenty or thirty-something professionals who have for years sublimated the desire to write and who are now willing to leave steady jobs, perhaps move across country, and take on more college loans even as they struggle to pay undergraduate debts, all in pursuit of the dream of being a writer.

The programs offer a haven, a place where there are no impatient parents doubting that this writing thing will ever amount to much, nor friends and relatives who think writing, unless you make it big commercially, is a huge waste of time. There are only other true believers, who just want to find out if the stories they can't shake, the promise teachers told them they possessed, and their confidence are enough to actually get an MFA, or, even better, to actually write a book.

The stories Carly submitted for my fiction workshops at Virginia Commonwealth University generally left her colleagues and teachers speechless. Where did these stories come from? How could anyone write with so much jagged-edged beauty? She was a tiny, tender thing, no more I guess than ninety-eight pounds, with a huge mop of red hair. She tended to fold in on herself as though shying away from too much attention, as though shying away from too much love. The stories were often set in places like the trailer park in rural Kentucky where she was raised by her grandparents, and they were about the scars we all bear, and peopled by characters everyone in the workshop knew. Good stories merely confirm that we are all blood kin in the same damned and often dysfunctional family.

I became her mentor. I often attracted students in the program who saw themselves in one way or another as marginalized, who had been denied the feeling that they were at the center of anything important—women who "came out" in their stories; angry political activists seeking to infuse their politics with the best writing they could; women in their forties, who didn't much care for the ritual of catching a few beers after class at a nearby bar; men writing about the fathers they had never known; foreign students. Maybe they didn't feel that they were at the center of what society said mattered, and identified with me, a Black woman writer daring to occupy the center of the classroom space with conviction. Whatever, they were often considered by everybody to be the most daring and dangerous writers in the programs.

Whether writing fiction or nonfiction, they wrote until it hurt and wrote because it hurt. They weren't ashamed of their demons or their questions. I taught them what I could, as much as anyone can, about writing. They taught me about life. Their narratives told me that color doesn't matter much in the end. In the inner city, people smoked crack; more than a few of my students were on Prozac, or some other legal psychotropic cocktail, needing it to get through the day and the night. They had been wounded somehow and were crying out for help. I was honored when they gave the class and me their stories to read, for we were being entrusted in a real sense with their lives.

With Carly and some others in the program, there was more than a little hand-holding and back-patting, as well as encouragement and listening. They had risked everything to enter the program and were filled with doubt. The program seemed so competitive, it often felt like high school, with certain people as prom queen and prom king. Some of the workshops had an almost toxic atmosphere, with one student telling me, "In some classes, there's the writing I do for the workshop, and then there's the writing I do that really matters that I don't share with the workshop."

The faculty would lead them into a sense of their literary voices, some crystal clear, blazing and beautiful. Some would become published authors of books; others would not live up to early promise. Students would find lovers in the program and divorce the spouses who had come to the program with them, gaining succor and comfort from the other writers, who were in the end the only ones who understood. There were Friday night readings where they read from their work at an art gallery near the campus. They would remember those nights well all their lives, hell, they'd tell their kids about those nights when they had been the center of attention, all eyes on them, all ears listening as they read their stories on the small stage at the front of the art gallery, amidst tables laden with stale tortilla chips and lots of red wine. These were readings where they cheered and clapped for each other like they were Denis Johnson or Colman McCarthy or Margaret Atwood or Lorrie Moore or Alice Walker, who in their dreams they were of course trying in their own way to be. It didn't matter that five years after graduating from the program, most of them wouldn't be writing anymore, according to a published survey of MFA grads. What did matter was that they'd had a dream, and they got to see if they could make it come true.

Carly was the blazing, nearly shattered star of the program, and several of us in the program loved her and held her confessions in our hearts and in our own ways tried to save her. Carly and I often had lunch at some funky café near campus or a coffee shop a block away filled with literary magazines, where lattes were served by art students from the school who worked there part-time. It was over those lunches that I learned Carly's story. She had a great storyteller's voice, jocular, bright, and in the midst of some funny tale about her grandma and grandpa, who'd raised her because her mother had "problems," she'd talk about how grandpa had touched her the first time and how she was afraid to tell anybody, hoping he'd never do it again. He touched her again and threatened to hurt her if she told. This went on for years. And even when grandma found out, she acted like she didn't want to know. Grandma loved her, and she kept making special cakes and pies for her like she always did, but wouldn't or couldn't make grandpa stop.

Carly was raped for years in that trailer until one day when she was fourteen, in a dream, God told her she could fight back. Resist. And she did. And she found her way out. Raised in a trailer park in Kentucky by a grandmother who failed to heed her calls for help and a grandfather who made her his sex slave, Carly managed to escape. She got out and thought she'd left it all behind. But there was no leaving it behind, not really. She had no boots, but found bootstraps anyway and attended college in Chicago, got a job as a paralegal, and after several years of working and writing at night, writing the stories inspired by all she had learned in her grandmother's trailer and her grandfather's poisoned grip, about how we live and love and suffer, she quit the job and applied to our program and was accepted.

She had been in and out of therapy. I once asked her how she had survived it all *at all*. "My stories," she told me. "Nobody would believe me when I tried to tell, so I kept writing, and it was like talking to myself, and I was the only one listening, and that was enough." Carly wrote no stories that she shared with the class about incest, but she wrote about everything else, stories that won her several awards and a prestigious fellowship while she was in the program. I'd leave lunch with Carly sometimes near tears at the thought of what she had shared. Before entering the program, for a year she had engaged in self-mutilation, cutting her arms, which explained the long-sleeved sweaters she wore all year round. After writing letters to her family at the suggestion of her therapist, in which she told her mother, aunts, and uncles about the abuse, the revelation was met with either silence or the charge that she was a liar. Yet I was inspired by Carly because she kept waking up to face another day.

I am convinced that the writing made each new day possible as much as her own stubborn will and the help of therapists. All the stories Carly wrote, the ones she shared, those that were published, and especially the ones only she ever read, weren't just a cry for help. Each word was a lighthouse in the dark. Reading Carly's stories, I often thought of Van Gogh's paintings and Anne Sexton's poetry, as both struggled with depression and suicidal thoughts they could not overcome. Yet there would be no suicide for Carly; she would continue to grow strong, marry, and continue writing, and I thought how miraculous that terrible crimes could nonetheless bring unbidden into the world such wondrous things as the words she wrote, and how those words created stories that saved her life.

The classroom is one of the most intimate spaces we ever inhabit. Despite the assumption that the distance between teacher and students is both wide and deep, or that discussions of ideas, philosophy, or craft are not shaped by emotion, the classroom is and always has been a venue where the most remarkable revelations of deeply held values and prejudices are revealed. Which students are called on to speak, which students are ignored, whether a teacher cites only the texts or offers personal views, and how students evaluate teachers all add up to a dynamic and ongoing group Rorschach test. Essays, research papers, poems, and stories submitted to fulfill an assignment can read like the pages of a diary. I always found final grades the most agonizing professional decisions I ever made because there was a beating heart waiting to know how I had passed a judgment interpreted too often as an indicator of self-worth.

When teaching in the "academy," I was that most unusual and unexpected specimen, a Black woman at the head of the class. Zora Neale Hurston's *Their Eyes Are Watching God* may be firmly rooted in this country's literary canon, but there remain hundreds, if not thousands, of colleges and universities where students can graduate without ever having a male or female professor of color. As a Black woman teaching in the highest levels of academia, my position as a theoretical and actual symbol of authority and expertise in the classroom broadened the definition of education and interpersonal discourse with new questions and answers.

While teaching at George Mason University, the "sister circle" I formed with Marilyn Mobley, Maxine Clair, Toi Derricotte, Mary Helen Washington, and Miriam DeCosta-Willis, all Black women writers and professors, helped me enormously.

Most of my experience in the academy has been at historically White institutions. And as in every other place in America where Blacks and Whites work together toward a common goal, race has been a subtext—a subtextual element that has influenced how my students, Black and White, perceive me and how I perceive them. I define myself as a global citizen and a feminist, and I believe that all stories are true, valid, and important, and that the most important skill I can encourage in my students (no matter what the class) is the ability to ask a question they had not ever imagined asking before. And I am ever aware of the responsibility and momentousness of *standing at the head of the class.*

I've had White students who could only see my natural hairstyle when they looked at me, an aspect of my appearance that they associated with fire-breathing political militants, or who could not see beyond my brown skin, which they may frankly feel remains alien. My White and Black students often came to me from rigidly segregated communities— segregated no longer by law but by habit, custom, and choice. For my White students, perhaps no Black woman had ever had as much potential impact on their academic lives and future careers, for I had the ability to pass or fail them. This reality made some uncomfortable. Yet most of what I have learned about how the seeds of racism are sown in White communities has been shared with me by my students. Everything I know about how and why Whites decide to reject that legacy, my students have taught me, with enormous generosity and grace.

I count numerous White men and women among my closest personal and professional friends, and among this group are many former students. These were students who signed up for my classes *because* I was the teacher, self-selected sojourners willing to read the kinds of books that encourage the ability to understand our shared racial heritage and break down racial walls, or stretch the concept of a valuable story, and learn how to embrace and hear the grammar and syntax of one previously described as "the other." Just think of it, all of us in a room together, Black, White, Asian, Latino, at a school like George Mason

University or Berkeley, writing stories and debating stories. Thoreau, Emerson, Whitman, John Brown, Paul Robeson, Mary McCloud Bethune, Susan B. Anthony, Black Elk, and Cesar Chavez would be so proud. For we aren't just interpreting a text, but cracking the codes of our potential greatness as a nation.

The assignment in my African American Women's Autobiography class was simple, cunning, and as I knew, scary. The memoirs of the poet Gwendolyn Brooks, abolitionist Sojourner Truth, journalist Patrice Gaines, political and human rights activist Ida B. Wells, and Black Panther Party member Assata Shakur were among the required readings. I wanted the class to hear these uniquely American voices, but I had more ambitious goals for the class. I wanted to create a space where the twenty-one White and four Black students could feel free to share the complex emotions of pride, anger, and confusion that the audacious lives these women had lived would inspire. I asked the class of twenty-five young women to write as their first essay a personal remembrance of a pivotal experience with a woman of another race. Their own stories would be the first, and for them, I knew, the most important text they would confront. I was certain no one had ever asked them to think deeply and write about such an experience. This was uncharted water, just the kind I liked. I knew that despite the persistence of social segregation, the lives of Black and White women intersected often, and that the altered racial landscape that these young women lived in offered them unprecedented opportunities to work with, know, and befriend their sisters in another skin.

I sat in my office reading the essays, laughing, near tears, horrified, gratified. I was overwhelmed and deeply moved by the authenticity and fearlessness of the stories the young women shared. A young White student wrote of being ostracized by family and friends when she brought a Black girl to church with her one Sunday morning, and how she had first learned to say the word "nigger" over meals at the dinner table. Another wrote of overcoming distressing stereotyped beliefs about Blacks when she worked at a jewelry store with a Black woman who became her mentor and friend. A young Black girl in the class wrote about idolizing the rock singer Patti Smith and how she was teased and called "White girl" by Black high school classmates. In their papers, the young women shared family and personal secrets; one family built a six-foot-high wall to separate their house from the next-door abode of a cousin who married a Black man, and another young writer wished she could find and apologize to the White girl she threw rocks at when she was ten, a girl she said she hated then for no other reason than that she was White and that she was convinced "had to think she was better than me."

We discussed the experience of writing the essays, how it had felt to tell these stories and to realize that they were not taboo or shameful, that they needed to be brought into the light, that they were as legitimate as the narratives we would read during the semester. This is the place where we began. I carry the gift of those stories, their precision and perfection, with me in every class I teach. Those young women trusted themselves, and they trusted the intrinsic value of the lives they had lived.

My life as a writer and teacher is interwoven and seamless. When I teach a class, I am speaking because my mother told me I should and my father told me I could. The classroom serves me as fully as my writing and becomes, like the writing, a sanctuary, a ground zero for the bold new act or thought, a source of self-doubt, pain, and creativity. To teach a class is to orchestrate the desire for knowledge and self-expression of a group of strangers who become a community. I've never really felt that anything I write was finished. I've never taught a class that didn't teach me how to teach. The best classes inform me not of how much I know, but how connected I am to the students who entrust me with their hearts and minds. In the classroom, we aren't readers, writers, students, or teachers. We are souls seeking, searching how to be, utterly, terribly, beautifully human. That's all. *That's everything.*

In the early days of Hurston/Wright Writers' Week, I gathered in a small classroom with ten or twelve Black writers from all parts of the country and sometimes the world. As we came together to craft and shape their voices and their stories, there was a sense that we were charting unexplored oceans of experience. We were creating spaces where the narratives of Black life, individual, local, and global, were respected, accepted, and honored. The complexity and diversity of what it means to be Black is the complexity and diversity of what it means to be human. Writing and discussing narratives separate from the White gaze liberated the writers in momentous and awesome ways. That same excitement permeates writers' workshops today at Hurston/

Wright, Voices of Our Nation, Cave Canem, and Kimbilio, where new generations of Black writers flourish.

Today I teach mostly in what I have dubbed the University of Marita Golden, online workshops in fiction, memoir, and the world of publishing. Black women who are in the words of one writer "old enough to tell the truth" register for my workshops in memoir. These women are ready and willing to write themselves into being, to write their way into beauty and truth. A Black woman on a mission is a proud Black-eyed Susan brave enough to stare directly into the sun.

CHAPTER EIGHT

A Calling, Not a Career

Sustaining a productive and emotionally satisfying writing life involves continuing to evolve and defining that writing life in terms that inspire strength and resilience. Within a decade of publishing *Migrations of the Heart*, I experienced an existential crisis. It was a crisis largely of my own making. The more books I published, the greater my dismay and disappointment. The pride I felt at having conceived an idea for a book, written it, and gotten it published was perennially sabotaged by the metrics by which I defined "success" as a writer. In the early years of my writing life, the "official" metrics of achievement, as I interpreted them, guaranteed that I would always conclude that I had fallen short of my goals. I had a career, not a calling.

My goals, and the goals of every writer I knew, were not only to write a book, but to write a book that was widely and positively reviewed in prestigious journals and papers by reviewers whose opinions mattered. That was just the beginning. Each book had to outsell my previous books, as though sales were a stairway to heaven. We kept our fingers crossed for interest from Hollywood, hoping for an adaptation of the book into film. And nominations for literary awards codified our sense of worth.

Everything in and about the publishing world encouraged writers to adhere to this toxic, too-often unattainable ideology. Sales of literary fiction, the kind I wrote and still write, are minimal at best, even with great reviews. The average well-reviewed novel by a first-time writer sold 1,500 copies back then—and sells 1,500 copies now. Only 0.4 percent of books sell 100,000 copies. Four million books are published in the US each year, and the continually shrinking number of reviewers can only review a tiny percentage. Those reviews often go to authors published by the Big Five major publishers, who launch a major media campaign a year before a manuscript becomes a book to ensure bestseller status.

For years, I knew none of this and didn't dare try to investigate how publishing worked. In my own eyes, I was simultaneously a success and a failure. My books were often selling three times the average sales figures for literary fiction or nonfiction, but to my eyes, the sales seemed paltry. I was convinced I didn't have enough readers, enough royalties, enough attention, enough awards. I was miserable, and I now look back with humor and grace and conclude I was also temporarily insane.

My books were favorably reviewed, if not widely, often in papers and journals read by people who cared about books. With each book, my fan base of book-loving readers, especially though not exclusively made up of Black women, and professors adapting my books for use in college courses increased. A few scholarly articles had been written about *Migrations of the Heart*, and more would follow. But in the boom/bust years of the early 1990s to the 2000s, the size of a writer's advance was what counted most among writers in the circles I was part of. Publishing companies, once small entities, were now owned by major corporations, and writers (even Black writers) began getting what we'd call "Wall Street" money for their books.

I was extremely productive, writing and publishing novels, editing anthologies, and having positive relationships with a series of editors at Doubleday who believed in me and were able to get me contracts for nearly every project I submitted. I had the same agent, Carol Mann, who gave me wise advice. With Clyde and I at the helm, the Hurston/Wright Foundation annually created and offered workshops and programs that supported Black writers. And yet if anyone had asked me then how I felt about my writing life, I would have told them I was unhappy and unfulfilled.

A scathing review of my novel *And Do Remember Me* was the turning point. On the pages of the *Washington Post Sunday Book Review*, the same space where *Long Distance Life* was listed as one of the best books of 1989, five years later I received the kind of review that had friends asking, "What did you do to that reviewer? Why was she so mean?" I had never before received a review that questioned my writing ability and seemed to imply that I had little to offer readers. Those kinds of reviews can happen to any writer: iconic writers, beloved writers, and required-reading-in-school writers. Most will at some point get that kind of review. I had gotten mine.

I felt pain, confusion, and anguish. Yet even in the grip of this emotional quagmire, I realized my response was a manifestation of a deep-seated spiritual misalignment. My mind was cluttered with the baggage of a dangerous set of beliefs about creativity, writing as a life, and the true meaning of "success." I knew I had to clear my head and my soul. I had to create a writing life and an attitude about my writing that nurtured rather than entrapped me.

I am not given to bouts of depression, but I allowed myself several days of flat-out sadness and quiet reflection. When I came up for air, I told my editors that I no longer wanted to be sent reviews of my books and that I had no intention of reading reviews anymore. They were shocked, because the breathless awkward waiting period for those first reviews is a time-honored yet deeply stressful ritual for editors and writers. My editors argued that they needed to send me at least a few reviews, but I held fast to my decision. My only caveat was that I would read and respond to any review that talked badly about my mama or daddy.

Writers are told that reviews sell books, but readers sell books by word of mouth. Libraries, bookstores, and book clubs, as well as radio, TV, social media, and the rest of the internet, are all part of the literary industrial complex that gets readers out of the house and into the bookstore, or gets them to order a book online. I was turning my back on the practice of defining myself, my state of mind, and my writing based on a set of random opinions, declaring independence from a custom that introduced the kind of anxiety that I no longer felt was inevitable or necessary.

All I could do was write the best book I could and then let it go, let the book find a new life in the hands of readers and the minds of reviewers and scholars. Gradually I stopped caring about the opinions of reviewers. I continued to read scholarly articles about my work because those essays were grounded in the intellectual quest to relate my work to trends in Black literature and the work of Black women writers. Scholars plumbed my work for meaning, symbolism, and themes and wrote about the multiple meanings of my stories, some of which I knew, others which they revealed to me.

The existential crisis that I was now working to unravel was existential because writing and publishing books to be read was so essential to my identity and my life's purpose. This journey wasn't just about my books, it was about my life. Soon I added periods of silence to my regular meditation practice. I'd spend weekends at silent retreats, or check into a hotel for "me time." In silence, I reconnected with the deepest meanings of why I wrote. I wrote because I had been "called" and "assigned" to write from childhood. I wrote because as I sat at my desk writing, either in longhand or on the computer, I often felt that I was committing an act of prayer, an act that made me stronger and wiser. I wrote to discover who I had been, to create who I could be, and because I believed that stories were powerful tools for love and healing. None of this had anything to do with book sales, advances, or reviews. I realized that I had a *calling*, not a career.

The writing was still hard, thrilling, a puzzle, a priceless endeavor, a question and an answer. Now I wrote with more passion and less pressure. And although in time I got everything I had once thought I had to have, I found I now knew those markers of success were gratifying, but that I could in reality have lived without them. More and more colleges and universities added my books to their syllabi in literature and African American and women's studies classes. My books became favorites with book clubs. I gained awards and recognition for my books and literary activism. I got a six-figure advance, and there was occasional interest from film producers. I spoke about my work internationally. I was a guest on *The Oprah Winfrey Show*, and years later, a question on *Jeopardy!*—two events that seem to impress people more than anything else. My work with the Hurston/Wright Foundation was considered groundbreaking and influential in opening the publishing industry to more Black writers. I think all that happened because I kept reporting for duty anytime I got an assignment from God. Writing was no longer the sum of my life; it was an expression of my life.

I've been asked about my writing technique and how I developed it. While I am scrupulous about craft, structure, and word choice, finding and listening for the voice of any story is most important. Finding that voice solves many issues of technique. From Alice Walker, I learned that courage is as important as the ability to write well. Watching Toni Morrison create a body of work that is scholarly and literary and that poses crucial, original questions, I witnessed the power of confidence as the foundation for narratives that can create seismic shifts in the minds of readers. Maya Angelou's books are proof that a life can be a masterpiece.

As an author and writer, I have been ambitious—*ambitious*, a word women, and especially Black women, are warned against using. *People will think you are not humble, it veers too close to the angry Black woman trope, you don't want to be seen as being too strong*, go the warnings. But I have written twenty-three books and cofounded one of the country's major literary institutions by being ambitious. I tell the writers who work with me to write for future readers of their work. Write so thirty years from now, you will be read.

I've known from the start that I was writing to expand the depictions of Black women, Black families, and Black life. My novels are rooted in stories of families in crisis. From the story of six generations of the family at the center of *Long Distance Life*, to the families impacted by a deadly police shooting in *After*, to the caretaking wife of a man living with Alzheimer's disease in *The Wide Circumference of Love*, Black families propel my work.

I write fiction to become a magician. I write memoir to take a stand or join public discourse and to continue the excavation of my life. When I wrote the memoir *Don't Play in the Sun: One Woman's Journey Through the Color Complex*, I found myself examining how my mother had wounded me because in many ways she was deeply colorist. Many of her stated beliefs and admonitions to me made me feel that as a dark-skinned Black girl, I was not loved or valued by the wider world. Writing that book, I forgave my mother for telling me, "Don't play in the sun, because you'll have to get a light-skinned husband for the sake of your children." I forgave her because a year's worth of reading, research, and conversations and interviews with Black men and women for the book informed me of how deeply that belief had scarred people of color all over the world.

I forgave my mother as I wrote each page because I remembered that it had been my mother who told me I was going to write a book one day and whose pride in the achievements of her little brown daughter was boundless.

I forgave my mother because she was the mother who helped make me a writer who could renounce the beliefs that had shackled her. But more than forgiveness, I grew to understand the forces that had made my mother both a proponent and a victim of colorist beliefs. By the time I finished *Don't Play in the Sun*, I had never loved my mother more.

I was "called" to write *Don't Play in the Sun* when my stepdaughter Keesha called one afternoon, saying, "Marita, I know you don't like those videos of BET (Black Entertainment Television), but there's one on now that I know you will like." I turned to BET in time to see India Arie singing the song "Video," an elegantly simple ode to the beauty of brown-skinned women and their worth. I sat transfixed and renewed by the lyrics and the video. And in those moments, India Arie unleashed my years-old but long-denied desire to write about the color complex. I sat in awe of her bravery in expressing in the face of perpetual resistance to the idea of brown or Black beauty the fact and assertion that she did not have to look like a light-skinned girl in a video to be beautiful.

Writing that book, as once again I fused my story with interviews, research, and profiles of others, I dismantled the dangerous and erroneous belief that light-skinned men and women were superior in all ways to those of darker hue. I simultaneously refuted the notion that those with light skin could not also be victims of colorism even as they benefitted from it. As I researched, I found references to colorism in scholarship, memoirs, history, and journalism, but no personal accounts like the book I was writing.

On many days, the writing was so challenging that I swore, after a few hours of writing, that I saw blood pooled at my feet. How, I wondered, could I write through the anger I felt about colorism and simultaneously shape a language that would heal and inspire? After *Don't Play in the Sun* was released, I received many letters from women and men of all hues whose lives had been defined and derailed by colorism. The letters came from places as diverse as Alaska and Algeria. Memoir again and again gave me *entrée* into the deepest meanings and understanding of my life.

My writing life has gifted me in multiple and wonderous ways. I've created stories that entertained and enlightened readers. I have expressed a talent that I was born to manifest. My books have repeatedly required me to renounce stereotypical thinking and opinions grounded in fear. In return, each story, every book has in different ways bestowed upon me an enlarged intelligence and vision that I try to regularly draw from.

***

Writing my novel *After* about the aftermath of a police shooting, I wrestled with what I was certain I knew about cops and what I learned about cops as I wrote. My son was a victim of excessive force wielded by police. My son survived his encounter with the police. Too many Black men did not.

I initially envisioned *After* as a novel about the impact of the death of a young man at the hands of a police officer on his family. The police officer was a secondary character. However, two years into writing, everyone who read the manuscript told me that the Black police officer in the novel, Carson Blake, was the most compelling character. My visceral emotions about the deaths of so many Black people at the hands of cops made it virtually impossible for me to imagine making Carson Blake the main character. Yet there came a point when Carson Blake claimed the story.

He claimed it because, as a cop who killed a young man he thought was holding a gun, which is revealed to be a cell phone, he is wracked with guilt and shame. The killing is ruled justifiable, yet his life is forever altered. This was going to be a difficult story to write. This was drama at its most complicated, and therefore it was the kind of plot that a novelist cannot resist. I realized that I had to think of Carson as someone who had been a child, who was a husband, who was a father, who had emotional wounds that still marked him. He was a cop. But he was much more than just a cop. He had to be portrayed as a dimensional human being whom the reader would have to feel sympathy for and empathy with.

One of my early readers reminded me that I was essentially writing a character study of a man in crisis. My interviews with over a dozen cops uncovered the complex reasons that they chose the profession as well as the challenges they faced in doing that job.

A rookie cop told me he had joined the police force "to protect my community." A Black female cop told me "We profile, we profile all the time. If we see a carful of Black males and they're pumping loud music, you better believe we follow them." A therapist who worked with the DC Police Department told me stories of officers who had tried to commit suicide after shooting and killing a suspect, and about the difficulty cops had in emotionally processing the violence, mayhem, and death they witnessed, experiences that led to post-traumatic stress disorder (PTSD). Most cops never fired their weapons in their entire career. One precinct commander told me there are no national standards for training cops, and as a result, rules governing excessive force are haphazard and inconsistent. A handful of bad or rogue cops commit most of the killings of people in custody, and police unions exert enormous power and pressure to keep them on the job.

I had to get to a place in my imagination where I could create a character who could kill an innocent man and yet not be demonized by readers. I took a year and a half off from the novel and wrote *Don't Play in the Sun*. During that year and a half, I evolved into a writer who could write a story not about a cop killing, but about a tragedy that leads to grief, redemption, and renewal. Upon reading *After*, Black readers told me they were surprised to acknowledge the humanity of the men and women "in blue." The cops who read the book thanked me for portraying them and their jobs with dimension and compassion.

My writing has been a passport to Jamaica, Turkey, Spain, Israel, and England for readings and lectures. Everywhere I traveled, the story of my people came with me, and the story of my people is loved and respected around the world. Among my most satisfying moments was the unveiling of a stand-up plaque placed on Harvard Street in Washington, DC, one that cited distinguished people who had been part of the Columbia Heights community. On the plaque was a quote from *Long Distance Life*, my novel set in Columbia Heights. That was the day I learned by reading another citation on the plaque that Jean Toomer, the author of *Cane* and a major figure in the Harlem Renaissance, had grown up, as I had, on Harvard Street.

One of my most profoundly full-circle moments came during an interview with the great historian John Hope Franklin. Franklin was one of thirteen writers I interviewed for *The Word: Black Writers Talk About the Transformative Power of Reading and Writing*. Franklin was the author of the seminal text *From Slavery to Freedom: A History of African Americans*.

I interviewed Dr. Franklin a year before his death in 2009 at his home, not far from Duke University, where he was the James B. Duke Professor Emeritus of History. Our talk began in the parlor of his home, located in Raleigh, North Carolina, and continued over a lunch of shrimp fried rice that he prepared. I entered the house starstruck, but Dr. Franklin welcomed me like family he had been expecting. John Hope Franklin was a dear and long-time friend of my agent Carol Mann's father. Franklin had recruited Arthur Mann, a fellow historian, to join him on the faculty of the History Department at the University of Chicago. Carol told me that as a child, she and her family and the Franklins had dinner together nearly every Sunday. The friendship between the two families was lasting and deep. And Franklin had introduced Carol to my first editor, Marie Brown.

Dr. Franklin and I were connected by several cycles of six degrees of separation as well as by our love of history. As we sat at Franklin's kitchen table eating shrimp fried rice I had earlier watched him prepare, I told Dr. Franklin that my father had told me about George Washington Wiliams, the true father of Black history in America. Dr. Franklin, who had written a biography of Williams, smiled and rose slowly, unfurling his lanky over six-foot frame, and went down to his basement. A few minutes later, I heard his footsteps climbing the stairs and then he stood beside me and held out an original copy of one volume of the two-volume *History of the Negro Race in America from 1619–1880*, published in 1883 and written by Williams.

When Dr. Franklin handed me the aged, worn, but still intact volume, which I held gently, afraid to damage its fragile pages, I thought about my father's stories, stories that had made this meeting with Dr. Franklin inevitable. My father told me that Williams had fought in the Civil War, had been a Baptist minister, a lawyer, a politician, and a journalist who taught himself how to write history. Few had heard of him, but my father had, and he ensured that I knew who George Washington Williams was. The spirit and the love of my father blossomed and enfolded me as I sat in the kitchen of one of the world's most important historians.

Over the years, writing about my parents and their role in shaping me into a Black writer has increased my love for them and my appreciation for how lucky I was to be their child. My father showed me how to set sail toward this world. My mother raised the mast. They were my first guides, and I have spent my life learning how to steer this majestic ship.

Appendix

Keynote Address

Delivered at the April 2021 Conference of the American
Society of Journalists and Authors

> *"A book is dead until someone reads the book
> and perceives the book in their own way. We
> give life to what we read. Once we finish, the
> book is dead again until somebody reads it."*

—Don Miguel Ruiz, author of *The Four Agreements*

When I was twelve years old my mother told me that I was
going to write a book one day. Her prediction was based on
solid evidence. I was a daydreamer, I wrote poetry, I spent
hours holed up in a kind of sanctuary I had designed in
our attic surrounded by copies of *Life* and *Look* magazines,
Reader's Digest, and whatever book, *Nancy Drew* or *A Tale
of Two Cities,* I was currently reading. I wasn't a particularly
obedient child; in fact, frequent punishments were the price
I paid for being blessed and cursed with an inquiring mind
that saw or imagined secrets and stories everywhere I looked.
But I did obey my mother's charge, her prediction, and her
baptism. I had no choice. I love books, always have. In 1962,
when my mother made her prediction, it sounded fanciful
and unlikely. I, a young Negro girl, growing up to write books
like the kind I read and adored? But by the time I graduated

from college a decade later, and with my mother watched seismic cultural and political change reshape the nation and my identity, the idea that I would become a Black woman who wrote books like Maya Angelou, Toni Morrison, Alice Walker, and Lorraine Hansberry seemed entirely possible—and not only possible, but necessary.

I have spent over forty years writing books and teaching other people how to write books. So literature and books are serious business to me: the air I breathe, the meaning of life, a home, an answer, solace, and a prayer. We love books and the journey they usher us into for many reasons. Books can be entertaining, plumbing the depths of our emotions. They can at their best produce empathy that gives us the courage we need to enter the world of those we have defined as the other or as different. Books teach us things that improve our lives. Books ignite our imagination and provide us with a new way of looking at the world.

All books don't accomplish all that, but the best books do, no matter the genre or the age or era in which they were conceived. But a book is at its heart a distillation of a process that all societies revere: dedicated thought, insistent questioning, a commitment to a process that requires a transformation of writer and reader; wrestling with big ideas; asking questions that are rarely asked, that are sometimes taboo, that have no definitive answer. Every time we check a book out from the library, as some of us still do, or buy it or even borrow it, we are endorsing that complex, difficult, yet for some of us addictive process. We are endorsing it and protecting it and encouraging it.

Books from the Bible to *The Grapes of Wrath*, from *The Miseducation of the Negro* to *Our Invisible Poor* to *The Second Sex*, have shaped political and social policy. Literature and books are sparks for the flame of argument and division. The best books are not wimpy; they take a stand, they stand their ground. We love books, and we need books. And yet we American and America-based writers do our important work against a dismal background.

I've come to this conclusion based on the statistical story of reading and of literature in America. The statistics are all over the place and are sometimes contradictory, but again and again, the stats told me that 21 percent of US adults are illiterate or functionally illiterate. 50 percent of US adults cannot read a book written on an eighth-grade level. A quarter of the population has not read a single book about anything in the last year. I was interested in when this precipitous decline in reading, especially reading literature, began.

The year 1982, the second year of the presidency of Ronald Reagan, pushed us over the nonreading cliff. That is when the levels of reading began declining steadily. Massive tax cuts for government funding for schools and other social services began the steady chipping away at our cultural infrastructure. Then there was the nationwide implementation of standardized tests which made billionaires of the testing companies and criminals of some teachers, principals, and test-takers, rather than learners of too many students. Students all over the country, not just those at inner-city schools, but rural schools, schools in Appalachia, schools in working class areas and the suburbs, are not taught to think critically or to understand that a required text can and often does speak to their lives right now.

The chasm between the enriched academic experience of students in private schools and public schools in wealthy neighborhoods and those attending the typical urban public school is vast. This divide results in a two-tier education system that determines students' success based on their zip code more than their test scores. Linking funding for public schools to property taxes ensures the persistence of educational inequality.

Then, many Americans are *aliterate*. A third of Americans graduate from high school and college and never read another book. They can read but simply don't. In a country of 350 million people, the typical sales for a literary novel or work of nonfiction are 1,500 to 3,000 copies, even with a *New York Times* review. A major literary award, depending on the book that wins, may bump sales by 10,000. And with the relentless, slow death of newspapers, the space for book reviews has shrunk massively. Americans work overtime to get more money if they have lots of it and must work overtime if they have little. The message seems to be if you aren't working like a dog, as the saying used to go, no matter your class, you aren't a real American. So who has time to read? Who reads more than anybody else in America? Sixty-five to seventy-five-year-old college grads who are retired or semi-retired, or engaged in work that is their passion and that provides them with a lifestyle that makes room for reading. And who in America reads more books than anyone else? Pew Research found that with the introduction of the electronic book (e-book), the person most likely to read a book of any type is a college-educated Black woman.

So the cultural, social, and political ecosystem that supports reading mirrors the state of the nation's physical infrastructure, as our bridges, rusting pipes, and polluted waters mirror and echo our middling, failing schools.

Ironically, Americans may not want to read or be able to read, but they sure want to write. In 2020, there were 1.7 million self-published titles: 1.7 million. Who are these people who self-publish a book that typically goes on to sell, if they are lucky, 250 copies? They are Americans who feel that they have an inalienable right to write, that their story is worth a book, a whole book, no matter how well or how poorly that story is written. They are writing their story for their grandchildren, for their children, who they hope will read stories they never got around to telling them. Those who independently publish are also fine writers, graduates of MA and MFA programs who despite their talent cannot get a contract with a mainstream publisher or a respectable small press.

Then there are the million books written annually published by mainstream and small publishers and presses. We are facing a tsunami of books that few people are reading.

So who are we writing for? You and me? Why do we continue to write when it appears few people are reading? Because books still matter.

The Power Broker, The Handmaid's Tale, The Color Purple, Silent Spring, How to Be an Antiracist: all are books that deeply impacted social policy and culture.

Those of us attending this conference live in a cloistered, nearly walled-off world populated by people who have easy access to books and the ability and desire to allow books to enlarge them. Yet reading books for pleasure and self-improvement has become an elite activity.

Books matter. Reading books matters. Reading a book stimulates deeper regions of the brain and activates higher levels of imagination than watching a film or video. That's why Bill Gates, Steve Jobs, and other titans of technology who made billions selling products that addict, distract, and depress the masses refused to buy cell phones for their children and severely limited their children's use of the products that had made *them* seeming masters of the universe. They were raising future leaders, not future consumers. For those who want to lead and make change, books matter. What books require to be unlocked and turned on to full power are the same tools used in innovation and invention.

And yet against this backdrop of declining reading, there is an explosion in writing, one activated by people's need to imprint themselves on the world and their communities, to speak after years of being silenced or told they had nothing to say. The explosion of writing in America is inspired by people's need to say *I am*.

Writing remains in the public imagination a high-status occupation shrouded in the mythology of glamour, fame, and riches. Even though I feel that the commitment of imagination, time dedication, and intellect that a good book requires is priceless, I can name a price, and it would start with six figures or more. All these American writers, many of whom don't read, know there is magic and a kind of wild salvation in writing a book. Americans are a bundle of contradictions, knowing that a book is hard to write but convinced in many cases that writing *their* book will be easy.

I am as you can tell by now a passionate, promiscuous reader. I read everything: poetry, nonfiction, fiction, journalism, social media, the internet, signs, and billboards, and I read films as I watch them for technique and meaning. As Oprah Winfrey always says, there is one thing I know for sure…and the one thing I know for sure is that writing a book is not easy, and reading a book is not easy either. I love books, and one of the reasons I love them so much is that they reflect and contain in them the flaws and imperfections—the biases—of their author.

They are expressions both of their social moment and the interaction of the author with that social moment, of how the culture as it existed at the moment of the book's creation made the writer a reflector of the dominant culture or someone who challenged or rejected it. And so while I am concerned about the decline in reading literature, I am equally concerned about the push to cancel and censor books that contain racist or sexist imagery or thought. How will we ever learn or teach our children the ways that racism and sexism are expressed in cultural products if we are terrified of looking at that expression dead on? Books are always being banned or canceled; this is nothing new. The current spasm of banning is merely a continuation of society's fanciful assumption that people's thoughts can and should be controlled and that there is one definition of what is harmful and regressive.

Writer Nashae Jones wrote a powerful essay for the *Huffington Post* titled "I'm A Black Mother and Educator. Here's Why I Let My Kids Read Racist Books." Until reading this essay, I was unaware that childhood staples like *Peter Pan*, *Babar*, and *The Little Princess* had been denounced apparently as racist.

She writes:

> Now, as a mom and an educator, I look at these books with a discerning eye. When I read the books with my children, we immediately discuss the book's period, the author's intent, and the harmful depictions of marginalized people. For my students, the majority of whom are white, I find it equally important to apply these same concepts.

> *Adventures of Huckleberry Finn*, a staple in our eleventh-grade English curriculum, has been on the banned book list for many years, but I contend that this is an important text to teach. Although Twain uses the N-word 219 times in *Huckleberry Finn*, there is a method to the madness. Removing the word desensitizes the horrific nature of the period. It delegitimizes Jim's struggle. Removing the book from the curriculum altogether serves as an erasure of history. It doesn't just erase Mark Twain's words, it erases Jim—the echo of the lived experience of so many American slaves.

Instead, I believe it's better to give students the tools to dissect and critically explore these types of books to ensure a healthy discourse. Furthermore, it is important to realize these texts are not vehicles of complete evil and that we can't just throw the baby out with the bathwater. It is more nuanced than that. After all, there is a reason Jim, an uneducated slave, is the pinnacle of morality in the Huck Finn text.

We need books that make us uncomfortable and that challenge us. We need books that we can argue with and question. The movement to allow college students to opt out of reading books that trigger emotional pain undercuts everything that a liberal education is supposed to instill. Reading the history of the discovery and exploitation of a world that was "new" to Europeans triggers sadness and anger in me; reading Louise Erdrich's novels of the lives of Native people in this country reminds me of the disenfranchisement of Black peoples. Books do that. Books make us feel, confront ideas, and think. We can be large enough to prevent a book or an idea from destroying us.

We can define the feelings that erupt when we read a book that we find harmful or painful as an opportunity to talk back. And just so we have some perspective here, in my estimation, war, racism, sexism, and all the other ways that people and nations are destroyed constitute the original cancel culture. The Inquisition, Female Genital Mutilation:

all part of cancel culture. White supremacy, Nazism, and even the banning of *Mein Kampf*: all part of cancel culture.

And so here we are: reading is an increasingly marginalized, nearly elitist, unsupported activity in a society where every other person wants to write a book and/or police the ideas in books. The impulse to police books and the ideas in them is a testimony to the power of books. We have a love-hate relationship with books that undermines their ability to do what books can do best, inspire us. How can we do our work as writers in such an environment? The way we always have, writing because the book police are coming. Writing because we are trying to create the narrative that a nation will feel they have to read, that they have to learn how to read in order to read. Writing because that is what we do and because we have been possessed down to our core by a story. Writing because we know in the end and in the beginning that the story is its own reward. The stories we create and dream can save us, whether it is the story of universal health care or of confronting and dismantling police brutality.

I once attended a lecture by the giant of literature Toni Morrison, a lecture in which she talked about craft and meaning and how she wrote her books. It was a lecture in which she read the opening paragraphs of three of her novels, and then, standing before a packed standing room auditorium at Harvard University, in her deceptively gentle yet steely voice, she critiqued, challenged, and questioned the original phrasing and writing. She then suggested to the audience revisions of the language that she felt would improve those opening paragraphs of books that were becoming accepted as crucial to our canon. I have never forgotten that. I have never seen another writer perform such an act. Morrison had the confidence, the will, and the heart to share with the audience the fact that art, ideas, and how we make them evolve and change, and should be submitted to scrutiny, especially by those who create them.

Morrison was informing us that a work of literature could be deeply affecting *and* rough around the edges, both poetic and stumbling. She was extending in that lecture grace to herself as the writer and grace to us as readers, if we would accept it.

I think that we writers have surrendered much of our power. We need to remind our fellow citizens of the significance of the book, literature, and reading, and why they matter. We've seen what happens when a country is so alienated from community, intellect, logic, reasoning, and empathy, all of which are fostered by literature, and what happens when those people elect a president who believes *his life* is the only story that matters—a president who reads the side of a bucket of fried chicken for pleasure.

Yes, social media, computer games, and all the new permutations of technology that are announced weekly have seduced much of our attention, time, and loyalty. But the story told orally, the book which gives the language of story a physical, literal home, literature which puzzles and expands us: this is the original virtual world. The hardback or paperback book remains a brilliant technology. You can sleep with it, and it doesn't emit harmful blue light. It doesn't need any charging other than your eyes on the page; you are the outlet. You can scribble in its margins. Its cover is usually a work of interesting art that you can feel and smell. Carrying a book makes you look smarter than carrying a cell phone.

I have taken my computer-addicted grandchildren to bookstores and let them roam and read aimlessly, making discoveries with no pressure to perform for their YouTube channel—looking for books that will perform *for them*.

I am no Luddite; I know the ways that social media has enhanced us, but we writers, we makers of books need to move past the polite, staid, conventional attitudes that have left journalism and publishing gasping for air as the internet stole their lunch and all their clothes too.

The work we do is too important to our society and the world for us *not* to advocate, educate, agitate, to inform our fellow citizens that our product, books, and stories and the experience they represent, the act of creating community and igniting imagination, is foundational for survival and growth. Just as the most dedicated scientists refuse to write off life on this planet because we as a species have degraded and deeply harmed our earth, our home, we writers must cultivate readers we have written off, discounted. We must push for the repair of the cultural ecosystem required to bridge the yawning gap between ourselves and the readership we deserve, the readership that will affirm the meaning of what we do.

Some Books I Treasure

I have had the tremendous fortune of having read hundreds of books, for information, for pleasure, for self-help, for uplift, to fulfill an assignment, and for the joy of entering a new world. Below is a list of some of the many books and authors that have broadened my sense of the power of language and storytelling in the hands of master writers. These are books that I reread or teach often. Please note this is a woefully incomplete list of the books that live powerfully in my memory and heart.

- The short stories of Anton Chekhov
- *War and Peace* by Leo Tolstoy
- *Their Eyes Were Watching God* by Zora Neale Hurston
- *The Ways of White Folks* by Langston Hughes
- *The Narrows* by Ann Petry
- The poems of Mary Oliver
- *Black Boy* by Richard Wright
- *The Bluest Eye* by Toni Morrison
- *The Trees* by Percival Everett
- *All Aunt Hagar's Children* by Edward P. Jones
- *All Over but the Shoutin'* and *Ava's Man* by Rick Bragg
- *I Know Why the Caged Bird Sings* by Maya Angelou

Resource Guide

Introduction

Despite an impressive increase in the number of books published annually by Black authors and the growth of online, virtual, and in-person communities of support, Black writers still experience inequality in pursuing the dream of publication, from lower advances and less publicity than their White counterparts to the absence of enough Black editors in the publishing industry to champion their work. This resource guide offers an overview of the resources that support Black writers on their journey of creativity and publication.

Books

- *How We Do It: Black Writers on Craft, Practice, and Skill* by Jericho Brown (2023)
- *Black Women Writers at Work* by Claudia Tate (2023)
- *The Anti-Racist Writing Workshop: How to Decolonize the Creative Classroom* by Felicia Rose Chavez (2021)
- *How to Go Mad Without Losing Your Mind: Madness and Black Radical Creativity* by La Marr Jurelle Bruce (2021)

- *The Sisterhood: How a Network of Black Women Writers Changed American Culture* by Courtney Thorsson (2023)

- *Women, Native, Other: Writing Postcoloniality and Feminism* by Trinh T. Minh-ha (1989)

- *Meditations and Ascensions: Black Writers on Writing* by Brenda M. Greene (2008)

- *This Year You Write Your Novel* by Walter Mosley (2009)

- *The Art of Slow Writing: Reflections on Time, Craft, and Creativity* by Louise DeSalvo (2014)

- *Free Within Ourselves: Fiction Lessons for Black Authors* by Jewell Parker Rhodes (1999)

- *The African American Guide to Writing Nonfiction* by Jewell Parker Rhodes (2002)

Masterclasses and Workshops

Permission to Write: permissiontowrite.com/masterclasses

Founded in 2017, Permission to Write publishes a literary magazine and presents writing master classes in genres ranging from romance to essays. Permission to Write also offers scholarships to attend their classes.

Hurston/Wright Foundation Weekend Workshops: hurstonwright.org/workshops/writers-weekend-workshops

The Hurston/Wright Foundation offers weeklong, weekend, virtual, and in-person writing workshops led by award-winning Black authors in genres from fiction and poetry to nonfiction. Graduates of the workshops include novelists Sadeqa Johnson, Nicole Dennis-Benn, and Tope Folarin.

The New York Writers Coalition Black Writers Program: nywriterscoalition.org/black-writers-program-about

The coalition regularly holds classes and workshops offering a range of topics, conversations, and lessons. Along with providing many free resources, they aim to create an accessible and inspiring community of writers. Many of their events are held on virtual platforms and are offered at no cost. The courses are limited to a specified number of participants and are offered several times through a series of weeks.

Kimbilio for Black Fiction: kimbiliofiction.com

Kimbilio's annual retreat is held each July at the Taos campus of Southern Methodist University. Their signature program facilitates writers finding their voices and honing their craft through culturally responsive teaching and through the nurturing support and mentorship of established writers.

VONA (Voices of Our Nation Arts Foundation): vonavoices.org

Since 1999, VONA has offered workshops for the BIPOC and multicultural writing community.

Retreats, Festivals, and Residencies

Retreats

Cave Canem's Retreat: cavecanempoets.org/retreat

Cave Canem was founded in 1996 by Toi Derricotte and Cornelius Eady to bring representation to Black American poets. The organization has hosted writers and poets attending the Cave Canem's Retreat at the University of Pittsburgh. Many of the fellows from the retreat have gone on to leave legacies in their field, and they include National Book Award recipients and poet laureates.

Wild Seeds Retreat for Writers of Color: centerforblackliterature.org/wild-seeds-retreat

Established in 2004, the Center for Black Literature brings together writers from diverse communities and geographic locations for a weeklong retreat. The retreat does offer a limited number of scholarships for participants. The Wild Seeds Retreat hopes to inspire new authors of issues facing the Black community and to offer them an opportunity to study in the company of professionals in the genres of memoir, fiction, poetry, and screenwriting.

Roots. Wounds. Words. Writer's Retreat: rootswoundswords.org/2024retreat-autumn

BIPOC storytellers are invited to attend the RWW annual retreat located in the Blue Ridge Mountains for a liberal arts style literary gathering. Participant admission to the retreat is based upon an application consisting of the writer's artistic statement, bio, and a writing sample.

Black Pen Writer Retreat: black-pens.com

The Black Pen Writer Retreat was created for womxn and femmes as a safe, community-based learning environment to expand their writing goals. Founded in 2022 by author Onyi Nwabineli, who desired a way to build upon the writing of intersectional identities, the retreat was originally based in London, England, but has expanded to international areas. Eighteen spots are offered for the retreat, creating a small and vibrant community; scholarships are offered.

Festivals

Black Ink Charleston: An African American Book Festival: blackinkcharleston.org

Based in Charleston, South Carolina, the Black Ink African American Book Festival works to amplify Black diasporic authors across the South and beyond. Started in 2016, the book festival works to bring together local Black writers and engage readers in advocacy. The main festival is held during Martin Luther King Jr. Weekend and is open to the public, although smaller author events are held throughout the year.

Black Authors Festival: blackauthorsfestival.com

Founded by Darlene Williams and Verdel Jones, the Black Authors Festival works to establish a community that supports current and prospective Black writers. The festival also has a strong mission to rid America of illiteracy, especially in the Black community. The Black Authors Festival takes place in Sag Harbor in Long Island, New York.

Harlem Book Fair: harlembookfair.com

Held in historic Harlem, New York, the Harlem Book Fair offers an opportunity to connect with fellow readers, meet influential writers, and dive into captivating stories celebrating the diversity of literature.

Kweli International Literary Festival: kwelijournal. org/2024-international-literary-festival-main-page

Created for BIPOC authors and readers, the Kweli International Literary Festival contains virtual and in-person events (based in New York City) to bring light and knowledge to BIPOC literature. The festival features readings, discussions, and masterclasses throughout the festival to promote BIPOC voices and inspiration to the literary community.

Schomburg Literary Festival: nypl.org/spotlight/ schomburg/literary-festival

Annually, the New York Public Library coordinates the Schomburg Literary Festival, which offers space for Black authors to share their literary works. The festival has conversations, readings, classes, and discussions with awarded authors.

Well-Read Black Girl Festival: wellreadblackgirl.org

The annual Well-Read Black Girl Festival celebrates Black authors and brings together authors and readers. A year-round book club and newsletter create a vibrant online community of lovers of Black literature.

Residencies

Chatham Emerging Black Writers-in-Residence Program: chatham.edu/academics/graduate/creative-writing/black-writers-in-residence.html

Residents of this program will teach a multi-genre creative writing course to students in the Master of Fine Arts in Creative Writing. The program, located in Pittsburgh, Pennsylvania, was created to nurture emerging Black writers and to support the teaching of creative writing. Resident participants will be involved in multiple readings and work closely with the faculty in the MFACW program.

Black (Space) Residency: blackspaceresidency.com

Guided by a small group of master artists and curators, the Black (Space) Residency offers support and instruction for creatives of multiple disciplines to continue their efforts on their subjects. Taking place in Minnesota, the residency lasts one to three months. Participants work with multiple institutions such as Berklee Art Museum and the Museum of the African Diaspora, as well as several others.

Anaphora Arts Residency: anaphoraarts.com/residency

This ten-day virtual residency offers tools for residents to engage with other writers and expand on their works. The Anaphora Arts Residency costs $2,400, although there are several partial fellowships available. The program offers multiple guest speakers and engagers, many of whom have been awarded by organizations such as PEN America and the American Library Association.

Scholarships

We Need Diverse Books Black Creative Fund: diversebooks.org/programs/black-creatives-fund

The Black Creative Fund was started in 2020 to support emerging and established Black writers and advance their works. We Need Diverse Books is working with authors to include more characters of color in literature, especially children's books, and established this program to sponsor Black authors. The scholarship will also provide workshops, mentorships, and author visits to recipients of the award.

Black Writers Collective Scholarship: blackwriters.org/scholarships

The awardees of the Black Writer Collective Scholarship will work with the collective to engage with the BWC Community and the programs that they offer, as well as receiving a six-month membership to the Black Writer Collective. A limited number of awards are given to the best application. Applications include writing samples and anticipated impact on the awardees' community.

EJ Josey Scholarship of the Black Caucus of the American Library Association: bcala.org/2023-2024-e-j-josey-scholarship

African American citizens of the United States or Canada who have been accepted to an ALA-accredited graduate program are invited to apply for the EJ Josey Scholarship. Applicants discuss in their application essays issues that are presently affecting libraries and how awareness should be brought to these issues. Awardees are given a two-thousand-dollar unrestricted grant.

Fellowships and Mentorships

Fellowships

PEN America Emerging Voices Fellowship: pen.org/emerging-voices-fellowship

The Emerging Voices Fellowship is a five-month virtual fellowship that provides mentorship and knowledge of publishing and literary agents as well as providing a creative space for new writers. They also provide community events with PEN America such as a year of mentorship, public speaking events, and a writer's toolkit to help new writers with their endeavors.

Epiphany Zine Fresh Voices Fellowship: epiphanyzine.
com/features/2021/6/1/submissions-open-for-our-
inaugural-fresh-voices-fellowship-2021

This fellowship supports one emerging POC writer who
does not have an MFA and is not enrolled in a degree
granting creative writing program. The Fresh Voices
Fellowship will support a writer of poetry and/or prose
with a two-thousand-dollar stipend, a close relationship
with the *Epiphany Zine* editorial team, and a publication in
Epiphany, as well as several other resources for emerging
writers looking for resources and guidance.

Kweli Journal Fellowship Program: kwelijournal.org/
kweli-fellowship-program

Candidates for the Kweli Journal Fellowship must
be residents of New York City, must not currently be
enrolled in a degree granting program, and must not yet
have contracted a book with a publishing company. This
program will provide editorial support to help the writer
to guide their works for publication in *Kweli,* participation
in four public readings, and an all-expenses-paid writing
retreat hosted at Akwaaba, as well as other resources
and support.

Mentorships

Black Girl Writers Mentorship Program:
blackgirlwriters.org/how-it-works

Black Girl Writers provides Black women the chance to
network with and be mentored by editors, writers, and

literary agents. This is a free program which organizes free writing events throughout the year. The organization aims to create a safe space for writers to share and discuss their current works and offers support.

We Need Diverse Books Black Creatives Mentorship:
diversebooks.org/programs/black-creatives-mentorship

The Black Creatives Mentorship will offer eight mentorships to Black writers. There are three positions for Picture Book authors, three for Middle Grade authors, and three for Young Adult authors. The winners of this virtual mentorship will focus on completing a full draft of their aspiring work and will build relationships to the publishing community of the United States and United Kingdom facilitated by introductions.

Black Boy Writes Media Mentorship Initiative:
blackboywrites.com/the-mentorship-program

Black Boy Writes invites all to apply to their mentorship initiative, where writers will be given opportunities to work with mentors of different backgrounds to develop community and support. Mentees will workshop their scripts in a monthly writer's room, as well as work with their fellow mentees on building connections with networks and production companies.

Permission to Write Mentorship Program:
permissiontowrite.com/mentorship-program

While also offering resources such as podcasts and masterclasses, Permission to Write also offers a mentorship program for Black and writers of color. The three-month program will have two meetings with your mentor across three months and access to three group mentoring sessions. Permission to Write, which has a strong focus on advocacy and creating, now has a literary magazine featuring the work of writers of color.

Foundations and Organizations

Hurston/Wright Foundation: hurstonwright.org

Started in 1990 by founders Marita Golden and Clyde McElvene, who shared a love of African American books and desired to promote and honor African American writers, the Hurston/Wright Foundation's mission is to "discover, mentor, and honor Black writers," and it does so today. The organization is named after Zora Neale Hurston and Richard Wright, both iconic literary figures. Since then, the organization has established the Legacy Award, which has greatly assisted with sharing the names of writers with large publishers. In 2022, the Hurston/Wright Virtual Writing and Professional Development Institute was started to help writers of all expertise levels to connect and work on their pieces with guidance alongside other writers.

The Harlem Writers Guild: theharlemwritersguild.org

The oldest extant organization of African American writers, the Harlem Writers Guild was founded in 1950 by John Oliver Killens, Rosa Guy, Dr. John Henrik Clarke,

Willard Moore, and Walter Christmas, all of whom were authors and educators. The goal of the Guild was to promote and create works that shared the experiences of Black authors and to create community within the 1960s Black Arts Movement. Today, they serve as great inspiration to many present-day African American writers who are still sharing their experiences.

African-American Writers' Alliance: aawa-seattle.org

Established in 1991, the African-American Writers' Alliance has chapters across the United States. They strive to work with and build community with new and published writers, as well as adding to their skills throughout the organization. Today, the alliance regularly hosts events and readings open to the public as well as members of the alliance. Those who want to be part of the alliance can reach out to request an application form.

The Black Writers' Guild: theblackwritersguild.com

Black writers across the UK contacted leading publishing companies to raise awareness of the industry's inequalities and the underrepresentation of Black authors, as well as of Black people working within the industry. These authors working to advance this cause formed a guild that works to promote their original purpose of including Black individuals in the industry. The guild has an annual conference and has established the Mary Prince Memorial Award, which awards authors for their work.

Lampblack: lampblacklit.com

In its work to support all Black writers by commemorating authors from across Black literature, Lampblack hosts readings, publishes a magazine, and provides direct aid for authors in need. The organization is committed to the advancement of Black literature and works to share voices from across the Black diaspora. They regularly host events that allow authors to share their work in fiction and poetry.

Center for Black Literature: centerforblackliterature.org

Founded by Dr. Brenda M. Greene in 2002, the Center for Black Literature at Medgar Evers College of the City University of New York has worked for decades to expand the public's knowledge of Black literature. The organization offers literary programs and educational resources for all, including conferences, retreats, and writing workshops. The Center for Black Literature works diligently with the community in both the public and private sector to produce events that share the works of Black authors.

African American Literature Book Club: aalbc.com

The AALBC website publishes book reviews and has profiles of more than 6,300 authors and illustrators, as well as lists of book festivals, events, and other resources for writers and publishers.

Black Writer Book Clubs

Center for Black Literature Monthly Book Club:
centerforblackliterature.org/monthly-book-club

Started by Dr. Brenda M. Greene in 2020 during the early stages of the COVID-19 pandemic, the Center for Black Literature Monthly Book Club was started as a way for Black artists, writers, and creatives to share their works and knowledge during the pandemic's restrictions. The book club was started by the Center for Black Literature, also founded by Dr. Greene. The book club meets regularly on Zoom during the last week of the month.

Mocha Girls Read: mochagirlsread.com

Mocha Girls Read was started by and for Black women that wanted to share and form community with likeminded individuals after its founder noticed many of the book clubs that she joined did not have many (or any) women of color in them. The group was originally started in Los Angeles, California, but currently meets on Zoom, and there are club members across the United States.

Your African Fiction Addiction Book Club: bookclubs. com/join-a-book-club/club/the-african-fiction-addiction-bookclub

This book club was started to create a community for individuals who wanted to read more African fiction. Members of the book club read African literature from around the continent and thrive on finding books that share the diverse literature from authors in Africa. Your African Fiction Addiction Book Club meets virtually.

Literature Noir: bookclubs.com/join-a-book-club/club/literature-noir

Literature Noir is dedicated to amplifying books written by BIPOC authors and that feature BIPOC characters. The founders of the book club work to educate and create a safe space for its club members. The members of the book club pick their monthly reads based upon a select theme and vote on the works that the club will read.

Classic African American (Black) Literature: bookclubs.com/join-a-book-club/club/classic-african-american-literature

Focused on learning more about African and African American history, Classic African American (Black) Literature brings people together to read literature that focuses on moments throughout history. The book club focuses on works that tell the story of African people and BIPOC individuals.

Black Power Book Club: bqic.net/black-power-book-club

Started as a place for Black LGBTQIA+ individuals to meet virtually and gain knowledge about queer, trans, and Black authors through literature, the book club was started by the grassroots community organization Black Queer and Intersectional Collective, a group that raises awareness about the liberation of Black LGBTQIA+ individuals.

Storytelling Toolkits

Black History Month Digital Toolkit: nmaahc.
si.edu/explore/initiatives/black-history-month-2024/
digital-toolkit

Created by the National Museum of African American
History and Culture, the Black History Month Digital
Toolkit was created as a platform for social justice.
The toolkit offers educational material that focuses on
literature and poetry, performing arts, visual arts, music,
and digital arts.

Freedom Papers Toolkit: tyreebp.com/freedom-
papers-toolkit

Organized by museum curator Tyree Boyd-Pates, the
Freedom Papers Toolkit was named after the eighteenth
and nineteenth century freedom paper documents that
declared African individuals free from enslavement and
oppression. This toolkit was formulated to disseminate
resources that share knowledge of racism and oppressive
systems in the United States.

**Antiracism Toolkit for Black, Indigenous, and People of
Color:** c4disc.pubpub.org/antiracism-toolkit-for-black-
indigenous-and-people-of-color

Started as a resource for BIPOC readers who are
navigating academic publishing and going forward
in the publishing industry, the Coalition for Diversity
& Inclusion in Scholarly Communications created
this toolkit. The toolkit not only contains resources

and digital material, but also an abundance of visual concepts throughout.

Black-Owned Bookstores and Cultural Centers

Mahogany Books: mahoganybooks.com

Founded online in 2007 by Derrick and Ramunda Young, Mahogany Books works to share books about and for those in the African Diaspora. Book clubs and conferences have followed, and in 2017, Derrick and Ramunda opened a store in South East Washington, DC, and have expanded to a store at the National Harbor in Oxon Hill, Maryland, as well as one at National Airport. Mahogany features author readings and festivals.

Pyramid Books: pyramidbooks.com/books

Located in Boynton Beach, Florida, Pyramid Books sells new Afrocentric books, many of which are small and self-published works. Because of this, Pyramid Books also works with local school districts and libraries to share works to promote literacy within their community. They also regularly assist with the planning of book festivals and events in the Florida area.

Source Booksellers: sourcebooksellers.com/about

An independent bookstore located in Detroit, Michigan, Source Booksellers offers a range of books that discuss history, culture, well-being, and spirituality, along with other unique items. The literary outlet was started by Janet Webster Jones, a retired educator from Detroit's public schools, and was originally founded in 1989, but opened its first storefront in 2002. Source Booksellers regularly hosts events and works with the city of Detroit to promote literacy in the community.

EyeSeeMe African American Children's Bookstore: eyeseeme.com

Pamela and Jeffrey Blair, founders of EyeSeeMe Bookstore, saw that children in their community were lacking in positive Black stories and desired to make a difference in this issue. Their products offer encouragement as they work to remove the cultural divide and promote literature that shows Black culture in a positive light. EyeSeeMe also works directly with the community, making African American reading mentors available and sponsoring events such as book fairs and literacy and culture presentations in the University City, Missouri, area.

La Unique Bookstore and Cultural Center: launiquebookstore.com/about

Desiring to bring positive and progressive change to his community, founder Lawrence Miles created La Unique African American Bookstore & Cultural Center. La Unique is also home to "The Poets' Den," where music and poetry events are commonly held, and provides a vibrant entertainment and enrichment space to the community in Camden, New Jersey. Besides providing books focused on Afrocentrism, the bookstore has reached out to other ethnic groups and readily shares information to their customers through literature.

Cafe Con Libros: cafeconlibrosbk.com

After traveling abroad and experiencing a community coffee shop in Ethiopia, founder Kalima DeSuze opened Cafe Con Libros in 2017. 90 percent of event and product proceeds go directly back into the bookstore, a key source of community in the intersectional feminist area in Brooklyn, New York. Cafe Con Libros values community, justice, and art, as well as respect to BIPOC and Black Feminist and Womanist principles.

Sister's Uptown Bookstore: sistersuptownbookstore.com

Janifer P. Wilson founded Sister's Uptown Bookstore and then Sister's Uptown Cultural Center starting in 2000 with the mission of providing resources for her community. She has also worked diligently to share the works of past and present African American authors. The bookstore, located in New York City, is a vibrant part of the community and a wellspring of knowledge.

Harambee Books & Artworks: harambeebooks.org

Located in Alexandria, Virginia, Harambee Books and Artworks offers a wide variety of goods such as books, clothes, and art while also supporting community interactions and activities in the Washington area. As Harambee means "working together" in Swahili, the bookstore shares merchandise from those of African descent in order to fulfill the need for knowledge and art in its community.

Marcus Books: marcusbooks.com/store-history

Founded by Dr. Raye and Dr. Julian Richardson, Marcus Books was created to honor activist and author Marcus Garvey and bears his name. The founders, who also established Success Printing Co., have used their platform to advocate for Black history and knowledge. Many of their books are by independent authors, and the bookstore works with poets and artists. They regularly host events with famous Black authors that inspire the community in San Francisco, California.

Literary Journals

Obsidian: Literature & Arts in the African Diaspora: obsidianlit.org

The magazine publishes emerging and contemporary work by both new and established artists across the African Diaspora in disciplines including literature, visual arts, sound, and mixed media.

Kweli: kwelijournal.org

With a quarterly online literary journal, year-long writer fellowships, multi-session workshops, writing retreats, individualized editing, an annual writers' conference, and an international festival, *Kweli* invests in the artistic and professional growth of emerging authors nationally and internationally.

Callaloo: callalooliteraryjournal.com

Dr. Charles H. Rowell founded *Callaloo* in 1976 at Southern University in Baton Rouge, Louisiana. With its emphasis on critical studies of the arts and humanities, as well as creative writing, *Callaloo* has emerged as the most essential and continuously published journal in matters pertinent to African American and African Diaspora Studies worldwide.

FIYAH Magazine of Black Speculative Fiction:
fiyahlitmag.com

FIYAH is a quarterly speculative fiction magazine that features stories by and about Black people of the African Diaspora.

African American Review: afamreview.org

African American Review is a scholarly aggregation of insightful essays on African American literature, theater, film, visual arts, and culture. It publishes interviews, poetry, fiction, and book reviews as well.

Black Publishers/Presses

Third World Press Foundation:
thirdworldpressfoundation.org

Third World Press Foundation, 501(c)(3), is the oldest Black publishing company in the world. Originally founded in Chicago in 1967, TWPF has been publishing Black literature under the direction of founder Professor

Haki Madhubuti for over a half century. In addition to publishing, TWPF runs a network of three charter schools. Now in its fifty-fourth year, TWPF is one of the last remaining institutions of the Black Arts Movement (1965–1975).

RedBone Press: redbonepress.com

RedBone Press publishes works celebrating the cultures of Black lesbians and gay men, and creations that further promote understanding between Black gays and lesbians and the mainstream Black community.

Just Us Books: justusbooks.com

Just Us Books publishes Black interest and multicultural books for children and young adults.

African Heritage Press: africanheritagepress.com

African Heritage Press (AHP) is a publishing house with a vested interest in quality creative writing on Africa and the African Diaspora. Its partnership with African Books Collective (ABC) of Oxford, England, UK, ensures that publications remain stable in major book markets with industry-tested distribution channels across the globe. Through e-book and e-marketing channels, no hamlet is left "unserved" with our dish of literary collections.

Conclusion

If there are additional resources that you would like to have included in further printings of *How to Become a Black Writer*, please email submissions@mangopublishinggroup.com. We would love to hear from you!

About the Author

Marita Golden is a veteran teacher of writing and an acclaimed, award-winning author of over twenty works of fiction, nonfiction, and anthologies. As a teacher of writing, she has served as a member of the faculties of the MFA Graduate Creative Writing Programs at George Mason University and Virginia Commonwealth University and in the MA Creative Writing Program at Johns Hopkins University. She was the first writer-in-residence at the University of the District of Columbia. As a literary consultant, she offers writing workshops, coaching, and manuscript evaluation services.

Books by Marita Golden include: *The Strong Black Woman: How a Myth Endangers the Physical and Mental Health of Black Women*, the novels *The Wide Circumference of Love, After,* and *The Edge of Heaven*; the memoirs *Migrations of the Heart* and *Don't Play in the Sun: One Woman's Journey Through the Color Complex*; and the anthology *Us Against Alzheimer's: Stories of Family, Love, and Faith.* She is the recipient of many awards, including the Writers for Writers Award presented by Barnes & Noble, Poets and Writers, an award from the Authors Guild, and the Fiction Award for her novel *After* from the Black Caucus of the American Library Association.

As a literary activist, Marita cofounded and serves as President Emerita of the Zora Neale Hurston/ Richard Wright Foundation.

Mango Publishing, established in 2014, publishes an eclectic list of books by diverse authors—both new and established voices—on topics ranging from business, personal growth, women's empowerment, LGBTQ studies, health, and spirituality to history, popular culture, time management, decluttering, lifestyle, mental wellness, aging, and sustainable living. We were named 2019 *and* 2020's #1 fastest growing independent publisher by *Publishers Weekly.* Our success is driven by our main goal, which is to publish high-quality books that will entertain readers as well as make a positive difference in their lives.

Our readers are our most important resource; we value your input, suggestions, and ideas. We'd love to hear from you—after all, we are publishing books for you!

Please stay in touch with us and follow us at:

Facebook: Mango Publishing
Twitter: @MangoPublishing
Instagram: @MangoPublishing
LinkedIn: Mango Publishing
Pinterest: Mango Publishing
Newsletter: mangopublishinggroup.com/newsletter

Join us on Mango's journey to reinvent publishing, one book at a time.